OZ CLA

250
BEST
WINES
WINE BUYING GUIDE
2011

PAVILION

First published in 2010 by Pavilion Books
An imprint of
Anova Books Company Ltd
10 Southcombe Street
London W14 0RA

www.anovabooks.com

Keep up to date with Oz on his website **www.ozclarke.com**. Here you can find information about his books, wine recommendations, recipes, wine and food matching, event details, competitions, special offers and lots more…

Editor Maggie Ramsay
Tastings co-ordinator and editorial assistance Dan McCormick
Proofreader Julie Ross
Cover & layout design Georgina Hewitt
DTP Jayne Clementson

A CIP catalogue for this book is available from the British Library
ISBN 978-1-862-05896-5

10 9 8 7 6 5 4 3 2 1
Printed and bound in Italy by L.E.G.O S.p.A Trento

The information and prices contained in this book were correct to the best of our knowledge when we went to press. Although every care has been taken in the preparation of this book, neither the publishers nor the editors can accept any liability for any consequences arising from the use of information contained herein.

Oz Clarke 250 Best Wines is an annual publication. We welcome any suggestions you might have for the next edition.

Acknowledgements
We would like to thank all the retailers, agents and individuals who have helped to source wine labels and bottle photographs.

Prices are subject to change. All prices listed are per 750ml bottle inclusive of VAT, unless otherwise stated. Remember that some retailers only sell by the case – which may be mixed. Please bear in mind that wine is not made in infinite quantities – some of these may well sell out, but the following year's vintage should then become available.

Contents

Introduction

Something magical happened in 2010. The UK Government gave a big, **fat, juicy chunk of money** to the UK wine industry. This has *never* happened before. I'm not actually sure that the UK Government has ever given money to *any* alcohol-producing business. But this year they gave a £380,000 grant to an initiative called 'Wine Skills' at Plumpton College, home of Britain's Wine School. The Wine Skills initiative provides tuition in sparkling and still winemaking, vineyards and grape growing, and business and marketing. These last two really matter. I've been out looking at our new vineyards round the south of England and I'm amazed and excited by their extent and ambition. But I'm very concerned about what they're going to do with all these grapes, and **who's going to buy all the wine**. Plantings have more than doubled in the past five years, and the Champagne varieties – mostly Chardonnay and Pinot Noir – have increased by more than 600% in the same period.

You can see why. Sparkling wine sells for a lot of money. Prices have been rising by a pound or two a bottle every year recently as wineries have genuinely struggled to keep pace with demand. The prices for Champagne-style English fizz range from about £17.99 to above £35. And the wines sell out. So far. The price of vineyard land in the south has more than quadrupled in the last few years. The French Champagne producers are keen to enter partnerships and to buy land. On a recent English vineyard trip, every vineyard I went to had enjoyed a recent visit from very **serious Champagne producers**. Champagne is all about money. They don't muck about. They must have been certain they could make money here. And the price of English grapes is mad just now. You can get up to £2,000 a ton for a grape like Chardonnay. Decent Australian Chardonnay is going for nearer £200 a ton this vintage. I smell a boom–bust. If English fizz is now £20 a bottle and we'll be seeing anything from three to six times as much wine on the market in a year or two, the price won't hold. We'll have to see cheaper bottlings. Maybe even distress-priced bottlings – and will those be of good enough quality to keep our custom?

The 2012 Olympics may soak up a fair bit. The 350th anniversary of **the invention of Champagne** in 1662 by the Englishman Christopher Merret – yes, English, not French – may help. But I fear a bout of re-adjustment is just around the corner. And it won't be pretty. A glut of English grapes? Yes. Welcome to the Real World, England. This year, producers can't get enough grapes and are paying some of the world's highest prices. Two years' time, you can't give them away and they're left to rot on the vine? And all those bright-eyed investment schemes go down the tube? It could happen.

Grape gluts. They always lead to tears. You can parrot on about 'those who do not learn from the mistakes of the past are condemned to repeat them' but wine people *don't* learn. Whenever times are good, people flood into the vineyard and winery business. You try to tell them to be cautious – they don't listen. It's a rising market; everyone's getting rich. It'll go on for ever. Does that sound like the last decade of our economy? But **nothing lasts for ever**, particularly in the fashion-sensitive and, frankly, not massively profitable world of wine.

Australia is the most obvious example at the moment. Australia virtually created our modern British world of wine; Australian wine – its lovely flavours, its fair but never cheap prices – made us all into wine drinkers. Exports soared, and from a standing start a generation ago, Australia is now the leading supplier of wine to the British market. Sounds fantastic. Except that this was achieved by deserting the great original proposition of over-delivering for the price per bottle and instead following a mutually destructive path of deep discounting and gouging for market share. Australia still holds top spot here – just. But at home much of their wine world is in meltdown. Already this year, 8000 hectares of **vines have been ripped up**. Experts reckon at least 35,000 hectares need to go – over 20% of the national plantings. The giant Foster's operation (Wolf Blass, etc.) is selling 7,200 hectares – much of it excellent fully planted land – for whatever price they can get. Constellation (Hardys is their biggest brand) is offloading $200m of assets at what people reckon is about 25% of their true value. Tim Adams, one of the Clare Valley's top winemakers, snapped up the famous Leasingham vineyard from Constellation for less than it would have cost him to plant it. The world-famous Roxburgh vineyard, producer of the iconic Rosemount Chardonnay of the 1980s and 90s, has just been sold to BHP Billiton. But they're coal-miners. Correct. The fabled Roxburgh vineyard is now more valuable for coal than for grapes. There's a surplus of 100 million cases of wine in Australia. It could be 200 million by 2012. And experts reckon that of the 2420 wineries in Australia, 2000 would **go bust if subsidies were removed**. Luckily you'll find quite a few of the high-quality survivors in this guide – still over-delivering, still in business.

But the boom–bust contagion can spread. New Zealand would seem to have followed an exemplary course of high quality, high price, and measured expansion. They almost got away with it, but Marlborough Sauvignon was seen as just **too much of a cash cow**. Money poured in. Plantings spread 30–40 kilometres up the river valleys, past where vines traditionally grew and, predictably, in 2008 and 2009 vast harvests produced – yes – a glut. Cheap Kiwi Sauvignon swamped the British market. It really hit home for me when I saw a 3 for £10 offer on Marlborough Sauvignon late last year. New Zealand exports were up 57%; they've now overtaken Germany in the UK. But at what cost? They still command the highest average price per bottle, but it's dropped from £6.58 to £6.05 in a year, and it'll be lower next year. Marlborough's hard-won status has been savaged in a welter of discounting. Grape gluts again. **Greed getting the better of experience**. And experts reckon that at least 300 of New Zealand's wineries are virtually insolvent. It takes a long time to build a reputation, and a very short time to lose one.

Will the contagion spread further? Well, the biggest offenders in grape gluts have always been the Europeans, in particular France, Italy and Spain. National governments and EU subsidies endlessly pull their **hapless producers** back from the brink. Argentina, Chile, South Africa and California don't have such avuncular governments, and California has seen several crises partially solved by wholesale ripping up of vines. Chile and Argentina are **in growth mode** at the moment, but so far quality and price have held. Indeed, Argentina has never been better, but as Malbec becomes a cult wine, the pressure will be on. South Africa is also in growth mode. But she had a majority of vineyards whose produce was distilled or turned into grape concentrate. These can be brought back into wine production at the bottom end, without distorting the market. Few of her upmarket wines have so far achieved cult status, and relative equilibrium reigns. Ah, cult status. A two-edged sword, but good can come of it.

If I had to guess where else **the fickle finger of cult status** threatens to point, Italy would be high on my list, for once – not for its world famous, or in some cases infamous, reds, but for its whites. No greater person than Italy's red wine king Angelo Gaja has said that Italy's next big success will be in white wine. Fiano, Vermentino, Greco, Ribolla and Arneis were his picks; I'd add Falanghina, Catarratto, Grillo, Garganega, Verdicchio – there's tons of them, mostly as yet obscure and afforded little respect in a world tiring of Sauvignon and Chardonnay. Their time has now come. And if you want to add a couple of red wine stars, throw in the fruity, scented Nero d'Avola and Negroamaro. Italy is fast moving away from an obsession with hard, tannic reds – and our drinking world is a better place for it.

Portugal is the other European country that is making equally exciting moves, yet so far cult status has eluded her. Mature Vintage port is one of the cheapest of all classic drinks. But it is the dry reds that are far **out-performing** their reputation. Areas like Douro, Dão, Tejo and Alentejo, grape varieties like Touriga Nacional, Touriga Francesa and Aragonez, give thrilling, perfumed, alluring flavours. Just as in Italy, hard tannic red wines are out, sensuality, daunting depth of fruit and originality are in.

Chile, Argentina, Italy, Portugal – these are countries carving a new reputation based on wines of originality, approachability and affordability. Wines for the real world. Our world.

Wine finder

Shiraz-Viognier, Bloodstone, Gemtree Vineyards, McLaren Vale, South Australia 49

Stickleback, Heartland, South Australia 78

Tempranillo, Clare Hills, Pikes Vintners, Clare Valley, South Australia 40

Sparkling
Jansz Premium Rosé, Tasmania 119

Sweet
Museum Muscat, Yalumba, Victoria 135

Viognier-Pinot Gris-Marsanne, The Noble Mud Pie, d'Arenberg, Adelaide, South Australia 133

AUSTRIA
White
Grüner Veltliner, Messwein-Celebritas, Salomon Undhof, Kremstal 52

Riesling Smaragd, Kaiserberg, Prager, Wachau 37

CHILE
White
Riesling, Cono Sur, Bío Bío Valley 85

Sauvignon Blanc, Leyda, Garuma Vineyard, Leyda Valley 66

Sauvignon Blanc, The Society's Chilean, Leyda Valley 87

Red
Cabernet Sauvignon, Valle Central (Asda) 102

Carignan, T.H, Cauquenes-Loncomilla, Undurraga, Maule 55

Carmenere Reserva, Falernia, Elqui Valley 21

Carmenere, Karu Estate, Colchagua Valley 79

Carmenere-Cabernet Sauvignon, Novas, Emiliana, Colchagua Valley 53

Malbec, Loma Larga, Casablanca Valley 35

Pinot Noir, Punto Niño, Laroche, Casablanca Valley 71

Syrah, Corralillo, Matetic Vineyards, San Antonio 21

Syrah, Costero, Viña Leyda, Leyda Valley 43

Syrah, Montes Alpha, Colchagua Valley 35

Sweet
Late Harvest Sauvignon Blanc, Concha y Toro, Maule 136

ENGLAND
Rosé
English Rosé, Chapel Down, Kent 104

Sparkling
Cavendish, Ridgeview, East Sussex 117

Cuvée John Inglis Hall (Seyval Blanc), Breaky Bottom, East Sussex 117

FRANCE
White
Bordeaux, Château Doisy-Daëne, Grand Vin Sec 22

Bourgogne Chardonnay, Domaine Jomain, Burgundy 54

Chablis, Daniel Dampt & Fils, Burgundy 32

Chablis Premier Cru, Côte de Lechet, Vincent Dampt, Burgundy 56

Chenin, Touraine Azay-le-Rideau, Pascal Pibaleau, Loire Valley 44

VdP des Côtes de Gascogne, Harmonie de Gascogne, Dom. de Pellehaut, South-West France 88

Cuvée Pêcheur, Comté Tolosan 98

VdP du Gers, Pujalet, South-West France 88

Graves, Château Le Chec, Bordeaux 64

Gros Manseng, Côtes de Gascogne, Domaine des Cassagnoles, South-West France 46

Marsanne, Pays d'Oc, Domaine de Corneille/Asda 99

Muscadet, Côtes de Grandlieu sur lie, Fief Guérin, Loire Valley 84

Muscadet (House/Sainsbury's) 99

Pinot Gris, Cave de Turckheim, Alsace 48

Puligny-Montrachet, Les Corvées des Vignes, Domaine Maroslavac-Leger, Burgundy 31

Saint-Aubin, F & D Clair, Burgundy 59

Saint Mont, South-West France (M&S) 70

Sauvignon Blanc, VdP Charentais, Domaine Gardrat 68

Sauvignon Blanc, La Grande Cuvée, Dourthe, Bordeaux 67

Sauvignon Blanc, VdP d'Oc, Averys Project Winemaker, Languedoc 39

Sauvignon Blanc, Silver Coast (Caves des Hauts de Gironde) 86

Sauvignon Blanc, VdP du Val de Loire (M&S) 86

Sauvignon Saint-Bris, Clotilde Davenne, Burgundy 68

Vin de Savoie, Chignin, Domaine Gilles Berlioz 66

Red

Beaujolais-Villages (Tesco) 91

Bordeaux, Château la Fleur Coterie 75

Cheverny, Clos du Tue-Boeuf, Loire Valley 34

Chiroubles, Domaine de la Chapelle des Bois, Beaujolais 60

Claret La Reserve, Bordeaux 76

Corbières, Château de Sérame, Languedoc 61

Côte Roannaise, Les Vieilles Vignes, Dom. Robert Sérol, Loire Valley 39

Côtes de Bergerac, Château Montdoyen, South-West France 40

Côtes du Rhône, Belleruche, M. Chapoutier, Rhône Valley 73

Côtes du Rhône, Mas Arnaud, Rhône Valley 58

Côtes du Rhône-Villages, Le Ponnant, La Ferme du Mont, Rhône Valley 71

Côtes du Rhône-Villages Reserve, (du Peloux/Tesco), Rhône Valley 92

Côtes du Roussillon, Domaine de l'Oranger, Roussillon 74

Côtes du Roussillon-Villages, Bila-Haut, M. Chapoutier, Roussillon 48

Côtes du Ventoux, La Vieille Ferme, Rhône Valley 90

Crozes-Hermitage, Cave de Tain, Rhône Valley 76

Cuvée Chasseur, VdP de l'Hérault 98

Gamay, VdP de l'Ardèche (Cave de St-Desirat/M&S) 100

VdP de l'Hérault, Grande Réserve de Gassac, Languedoc-Roussillon 76

Minervois La Livinière, Domaine des Garennes, Gérard Bertrand, Languedoc-Roussillon 36

Pécharmant, Château de Tiregand, South-West France 59

Saint-Chinian, 'Les Fleurs Sauvages', Château de Combebelle, Languedoc 61

Saint-Joseph Les Coteaux, Eric & Joel Durand, Rhône Valley 35

Saint-Joseph, Nicolas-Perrin, Rhône Valley 53

Syrah, Ardèche, Vignerons Ardéchois, Rhône Valley 93

Syrah-Merlot VdP d'Oc, Reserve de l'Aube, Père Anselme, Languedoc 81

Vacqueyras, Carmin Brillant, Le Clos de Caveau, Rhône Valley 54

Ventoux, Domaine des Anges, Rhône Valley 57

Rosé

Coteaux d'Aix-en-Provence Rosé, La Chapelle, Château Pigoudet, Provence 105

Coteaux du Languedoc Rosé, Les Arbousiers, Languedoc 106

Côtes de Provence, Château Saint Baillon, Provence 105

Merlot-Cabernet Sauvignon, Liboreau, VdP Charentais 107

Pinot Rosé, Pays d'Oc, Domaine Begude, Languedoc 106

Rosé de la Chevalière, VdP d'Oc, Laroche, Languedoc 106

Sparkling

Champagne, Blanc de Blancs, Cuis 1er Cru, Pierre Gimonnet & Fils 115

Champagne, Blanc de Blancs Grand Cru, Le Mesnil 114

Champagne Brut Réserve, Charles Heidsieck 114

Champagne, Brut Special Reserve (P & C Heidsieck/Waitrose) 116

Champagne, Brut Tradition, Marc Chauvet 118

Champagne, Esprit Brut, Henri Giraud 115

Champagne, Les Pionniers (P & C Heidsieck/Co-op) 116

Crémant de Bourgogne Brut Rosé, Blason de Bourgogne (Caves Bailly Lapierre) 118

Crémant de Loire, Pascal Pibaleau 119

Crémant du Jura, Chardonnay Brut,
  Philippe Michel 121
Vintage Champagne (Union
  Champagne/Tesco) 117

Sweet

Gaillac Doux, Renaissance, Domaine
  Rotier, South-West France 133
Monbazillac, Château Vari, South-
  West France 136
Sauternes, Château
  Suduiraut/Waitrose, Bordeaux 134

GERMANY
White

Riesling, Bassermann-Jordan, Pfalz 26
Riesling, Dr Wagner, Mosel 26
Riesling Spätlese, Kreuznacher
  Krötenpfuhl, Dönnhoff, Nahe 58

Red

Dornfelder Trocken, Kollmann-Lex,
  Mosel 52

GREECE
Red

Cabernet Sauvignon, Tsantali,
  Halkidiki 75

Sweet

Voudomato, Hatzidakis, Santorini 132

HUNGARY
White

Cserszegi Füszeres, Hilltop
  Neszmély 98
Eva's Vineyard, Hilltop Neszmély
  99
Furmint, Patricius, Tokaji 54

ITALY
White

Blanc de Morgex et de La Salle,
  'Rayon', La Cave du Vin Blanc de
  Morgex et de La Salle, Valle d'Aosta
  26
Collio Goriziano, Clivi Brazan, I Clivi di
  Ferdinando Zanusso, Friuli 60
Grillo, Italia, Sicily 85
Falanghina, Giardini, Puglia 69
Falanghina, Terredora, Campania 65
Polena, Donnafugata, Sicily 28
Saluti Vino da Tavola 88
Soave, Pieropan, Veneto 37
Soave Classico, Monte Fiorentine,
  Ca'Rugate, Veneto 36
Veltliner, Eisacktal, Peter Pliger, Alto
  Adige 38
Vermentino, Lunae, Colli di Luni,
  Lunae Bosoni, Liguria 44
Vernaccia di San Gimignano, Le
  Calcinaie, Tuscany 64

Red

Amarone della Valpolicella, Rocca
  Alata (Cantina di Soave/Tesco),
  Veneto 47
Amarone della Valpolicella (Cantina
  Valpantena/Sainsbury's), Veneto 38
Cacc'e Mmitte di Lucera,
  Pezzagrande, Masseria Celentano,
  Puglia 74
Langhe, Suagnà, Bricco Rosso,
  Piedmont 89
Negramaro del Salento, Pietraluna,
  Racemi, Puglia 80
Nero d'Avola, Terre dell'Isola, Sicily 93
Nero d'Avola-Syrah, AgroGento, Sicily
  90
Rosso, Trinacria, Sicily 101
Valpolicella, Allegrini, Veneto 72

Sparkling

Bellante, Brut Rosé (Bonotto/M&S)
  120
Lambrusco dell'Emilia, Camillo Donati
  121
Moscato-Freisa (M&S) 120
Prosecco, Il Fresco, Villa Sandi 120

NEW ZEALAND
White

Chardonnay, Opou Vineyard, Millton,
  Gisborne 43
Sauvignon Blanc, Cape Crest, Te
  Mata Estate, Hawkes Bay 33
Sauvignon Blanc, Clifford Bay, Villa
  Maria, Marlborough 25
Sauvignon Blanc, Greenhough,
  Nelson 64
Sauvignon Blanc, Tinpot Hut,
  Marlborough 50

Red

Gamay Noir, Te Mata Estate, Hawkes Bay 58

Pinot Noir, Gunboat Point, Central Otago 50

Pinot Noir, Marlborough (Asda) 73

Pinot Noir, Palliser Estate, Martinborough 38

Pinot Noir, Paper Road, Borthwick Vineyard, Wairarapa 46

Syrah, Sacred Hill, Hawkes Bay 56

Syrah, Vidal, Hawkes Bay 41

Sparkling

Deutz Marlborough Cuvée Brut 119

Pelorus, Cloudy Bay 116

Sweet

Noble Sauvignon Blanc, The Ned, Marlborough 134

Riesling, Sweet Agnes, Seifried Estate, Nelson 132

PORTUGAL
White

Terras do Sado, Nico, Pegões co-op, Setúbal Peninsula 87

Vinho Verde, Quinta de Azevedo, Sogrape 46

Red

Dão (Tesco) 94

Douro, La Rosa Reserve, Quinta de la Rosa 27

Douro Reserva, Quinta de la Rosa/Waitrose 45

Douro (Quinta do Crasto/Sainsbury's) 79

Syrah-Aragonês-Alicante, Valoroso, Casa Ermelinda Freitas, Península de Setúbal 78

Vinho Verde Tinto, Afros Vinhão 32

Rosé

Dão, Touriga Nacional Rosé, Quinta da Falorca, Quinta Vale das Escadinhas 104

Fortified

Madeira, Full Rich, Henriques & Henriques 126

Pink Port, Croft 129

Pink Port (Marks & Spencer) 129

Port, Graham's Crusted 128

Port, Terra Prima Reserve, Fonseca 129

Port, Warre's Late Bottled Vintage 128

Ruby Port (Asda) 129

Ruby Port (Sainsbury's) 129

Tawny Porto, Colheita, Cálem 127

Vintage Port, Fonseca Guimaraens 127

Vintage Port (Symington Family Estates/Tesco) 128

Sweet

Moscatel de Setúbal, Bacalhôa 135

SLOVENIA
White

Riesling, Verus, Stajerska 67

SOUTH AFRICA
White

Chardonnay, Vredenhof Cellar Reserve, Western Cape 85

Chenin Blanc, Bush Vine, Zalze, Kleine Zalze 84

Chenin Blanc, The Den, Painted Wolf, Coastal Region 65

Chenin Blanc, Secateurs, Badenhorst Family Wines, Swartland 67

Sauvignon Blanc, Cederberg 41

Sauvignon Blanc, De Grendel, Coastal Region 65

Sauvignon Blanc, Ormonde Cellars/Tesco, Darling 70

Sauvignon Blanc, Six Hats, Fairtrade 70

Red

Cabernet Sauvignon, Douglas Green, Western Cape 91

Cabernet Sauvignon, Six Hats, Fairtrade 81

Cabernet Sauvignon-Merlot, Mill Race, Vergelegen, Stellenbosch 71

Pinotage, Beyers Truter/Tesco, Stellenbosch 78

Pinotage, Swartland Winery/Tesco 95

Shiraz, Six Hats, Fairtrade 81

Shiraz-Merlot, Fairhills, Western Cape 90

Rosé

Rosé, Boschendal, Coastal Region
106

SPAIN
White

Rueda Verdejo, Carrasviñas, Bodegas
Félix Lorenzo Cachazo, Castilla y
León 69

Red

Empordá, Sauló, Espelt, Catalunya 31
Garnacha, Borsao, Campo de Borja
92
Garnacha, Gran Tesoro, Campo de
Borja 101
Garnacha-Tempranillo, Gran López,
Campo de Borja 95
Jumilla, Carchelo, Bodegas Carchelo,
Murcia 61
Mencía, Gaba do Xil, Telmo
Rodríguez, Valdeorras 30
Priorat, Coma Vella, Mas d'en Gil,
Catalunya 27
Priorat, Salanques, Mas Doix,
Catalunya 23
Ribera del Duero, El Lagar de Isilla,
Castilla y León 51
Ribera del Duero Crianza, Viña
Pedrosa, Bodegas Pérez Pascuas,
Castilla y León 28
Ribera del Duero, Psi, Dominio de
Pingus, Castilla y León 33
Rioja, Amenital, Bodegas Miguel
Ángel Muro 24
Rioja, Single Vineyard, Ramón Bilbao
74
Rioja, Vega Ariana 94
Rioja Reserva, Viña Arana, La Rioja
Alta 30
Tempranillo, Sabina, Navarra 95
Tempranillo, Utiel Requena, Toro
Loco, Valencia 102
Tempranillo-Shiraz, Vino de la Tierra
de Castilla y León, Storks' Tower,
Antonio Barceló 80
Utiel Requena, Viña Decana Reserva,
Valencia 94

Rosé

Somontano, Tempranillo-Cabernet
Sauvignon, Bestué, Otto Bestué
104
Utiel Requena, Toro Loco Rosé,
Valencia 107

Sparkling

Vintage Cava (Codorníu/Sainsbury's)
121

Sweet

Málaga, Seleccion Especial, Jorge
Ordoñez 132

Fortified

Dry Amontillado, Lustau/Sainsbury's
Taste the Difference 125
Fino del Puerto Sherry, Solera
Jerezana (Waitrose) 125
Manzanilla, La Gitana, Hidalgo 124
Manzanilla (Williams & Humbert/
Marks & Spencer) 126
Dry Oloroso, Lustau/Sainsbury's Taste
the Difference 125
Viejo Oloroso Dulce Sherry, The
Society's Exhibition (Sanchez
Romate) 124

USA
White

Viognier, Zaca Mesa, Santa Ynez
Valley, California 55

Red

Cabernet Sauvignon, Robert Mondavi
Winery, Napa Valley, California 30
Cabernet Sauvignon, Steak House,
The Magnificent Wine Company,
Columbia Valley, Washington 72
Small Berry Mourvèdre, Cline, Contra
Costa County, California 29
Old Vine Zinfandel, Ravenswood,
Lodi, California 57

Rosé

Zinfandel Rosé (House/Sainsbury's)
107

TOP
250

TOP 100

Boy, do we need to drink some decent wine this year. Not just OK wine, not just pleasant and inoffensive wine, but wine pulsing with passion and optimism and personality. Each time I open a newspaper and read of service cuts and tax rises, some already implemented and many others looking as though they'll be breeding and multiplying for years yet, I feel my hand reaching to the wine rack in search of solace and encouragement. With that in mind I've decided to give you my Top 100 wines this year. For the past few years I've picked a Top 50, but there is always a whole raft of exciting, energizing wines that I have to leave out, wines that could play their part in making us all feel just a bit more sure of our place in the world amid the chaos and crisis that still threaten us. These wines are ones that speak to my spirit, to my soul. They're not safe and predictable, they don't mutter, they sing and shout. From the zesty and refreshing to the grand and majestic, they have a mission – to taste great and give pleasure and sustenance in difficult times.

This chapter lists my favourite wines of the year, both red and white:

🍷 = red wine 🍷 = white wine

1 2007 Shiraz, Tim Adams, Clare Valley, South Australia, 14.5% abv

AustralianWineCentre.co.uk, Tesco, £11.29

I've tasted and drunk this wine a number of times this year – not just because I like it, but because I keep having to prove to myself it really is as good as it seems. Did I just have one supreme bottle; will the others all be more pedestrian? So I try again, and as the level of the wine in the glass sinks, the perfume and personality soar. If I'm in winetasting mood, I keep on adjusting my score upwards; if I'm in drinking mood, the smile on my face just gets broader and broader. I simply can't think of another wine that matches beauty and power in the same way, that offers up immensely rich fruit, yet doesn't smash it with too much oak or scar it with too much tannin. The texture of this wine is like velvet – an overused phrase, but this time it's true. The flavours wash over your tongue, they caress your palate and linger long after you've swallowed. And those flavours? Sweet mint leaves, lush blackberry, finely focused blackcurrants rubbed with eucalyptus oil, all this in a cocoon of coconut and chocolate cream.

2 2008 Cabernet Sauvignon-Merlot, Moda, Joseph, Primo Estate, McLaren Vale, South Australia, 14.5% abv

AustralianWineCentre.co.uk, £25

I remember moaning a few years ago that I only ever drank young Moda, yet the quality and flavour were so full of promise I just knew it would be even better with age. The message got through. Earlier this year a box arrived on my doorstep with a clutch of Moda bottles going back to 1992. I was so excited I opened them all to drink during the England–Ireland rugby game – a feast for all the senses, I hoped. The rugby was dull, the wines heavenly. Interestingly, the earlier Modas did need aging to soften up and open out, but there's been a sea change in grape sources and style in the past few years and, although they will age brilliantly, they're simply fantastic to drink at two or three years old. The 2008 is as dense as wine can be, thrillingly bitter-sweet as only the best dark chocolate can manage and yet the bitterness shares space with coconut scented with chocolate dust and ripe black plums halfway to syrup. But the syrup is black treacle swirled together with licorice and resinous herbs. The bitterness. The sweetness. The fundamental excellence.

3   2008 Syrah, Corralillo, Matetic Vineyards, San Antonio, Chile, 14.5% abv
🍷 Oddbins, £16.99

Chile hasn't been making Syrah for very long, but it is turning out some startlingly original wines, many of them from brand new coastal regions like Elqui, Limarí or, in this case, San Antonio. This wine was so dark and purple, the glass I tasted it from was stained an hour after I'd left it. And it smelt sensational, not with a blockbuster, brow-beating power, but with a well-fed, sensual beauty that carried over into its taste. There *is* tannin there and this will help the wine to age to a memorable maturity in five years or more, but any roughness is drowned by the flood of rich blackberry, damson and morello cherry fruit, by the smoky chocolate sweetness which could all be too much of a good thing, until up comes a perfume of black peppercorns and green leaves that coats the ripeness and calms the rush of ripe fruit.

4   2006 Carmenere Reserva, Falernia, Elqui Valley, Chile, 14.5% abv
🍷 Cambridge Wine Merchants, Great Western Wine, Harvey Nichols, Tanners, £11.25

Whoever said that Chile was like a Volvo – solid, reliable – must be eating their words now. New, exciting areas keep springing out of the shadows and the wine map is becoming peppered with place names that simply didn't exist a few years ago. The Elqui Valley, up towards the Atacama desert, used to grow grapes for distillation into the local firewater. Far too hot for table wine, they said. It took an itinerant Swiss guy to say it's not too hot – sunny, yes, but there are fierce sea gales howling up the valley every day which actually make it colder than areas further south. The mixture of strong sun and cold winds produces amazingly focused, pinpoint-clear fruit flavours in the wines and this example shows what a brilliantly original grape Carmenère is. It's almost absurdly ripe, the blackcurrant and damson fruit pulsating with concentrated sweetness, but that's matched by a savoury streak of black peppercorn, soy sauce, graphite minerality and leafy freshness that spirals through the wine and ensures, above all, its utter drinkability.

5   2007 Château Doisy-Daëne, Grand Vin Sec, Bordeaux, France, 12.5% abv
♀ Tanners, £15.50, Wine Society, £16

To anyone who says 'I don't like Sauvignon', I reply – 'try this'. It's 100% Sauvignon, which is rare in Bordeaux, where Sauvignon is usually blended with Sémillon. But this wine is an even greater rarity because Doisy-Daëne is a Sauternes property, famous for sweet wine – and this doesn't have a gram of sugar in it. What it does have is an explosion of flavours as fascinating as any in France. It bursts with the taste of ripe nectarine and crisp English eating apples. It gains weight and succulence from its time in oak barrels and this gives me a childhood memory of custard burnt very slightly at the edges and walnut bread. Add some leafy acidity and smoky coffee cream richness and you're in the presence of a true original.

6   2008 Semillon, Tim Adams, Clare Valley, South Australia, 13.5% abv
♀ AustralianWineCentre.co.uk, Tesco, £10.29

I don't know how he does it. Tim Adams' 2007 Semillon seemed just about as good as it could get. Then along comes the 2008 and it's even more delicious. And I've just had a sneak preview of the 2009, and, dammit, it's going to be better still. So when this runs out, no tears please, switch seamlessly to the 2009. The 2008 is a brilliant mixture of richness, fruit and spice. The fruit's based on apples – ripe cooking apples, apple pie, apple cake, apple turnovers, with a little cooked orange and lemon peel to gee it up. The richness is custard, like the sweet, spicy cinnamon and nutmeg custard you get in a bread and butter pudding. Drink it? I could eat it.

7   2005 Priorat, Salanques, Mas Doix, Catalunya, Spain, 15% abv
🍷 Justerini and Brooks, £29.40

I used to find Priorat just too much of a good thing. Traditionally it was an enormous beast grown in the wild hills south-west of Barcelona that garnered heaps of praise and tons of high marks from the critics, but I'm not sure how much pleasure it gave. Certainly I found the stuff virtually stuck to my teeth. But the past few years have seen a sea change as an army of newcomers arrived and started challenging preconceptions. Now it's just as rich as of old, just as overripe and baked on the vine, but also much more balanced and, well, drinkable. It has a powerful taste of dates and sun-shrivelled grapes mingling with stewed black cherries, honey and chocolate. Lovely overripeness matched by truly ripe sweet fruit allows the wine to be dense, muscular and splendid.

8   2008 Chardonnay, Clonale, Kooyong, Mornington Peninsula, Victoria, Australia, 13% abv
🍷 Cambridge Wine Merchants, Great Western Wine, Philglas & Swiggot, £15.95

Australian Chardonnay is such a beautiful wine when it's properly done. Australia didn't become famous for Chardonnay for no reason: she literally reinvented the way Chardonnay should be grown and made into wine, and in doing so created a whole new raft of possibilities for this excellent grape. It all went wrong when the global brands in California and Australia and the supermarkets in the UK decided that Chardonnay was a golden goose that simply couldn't lay golden eggs fast enough to keep up with their greed. So there are now an awful lot of people who put their finger down their throat on hearing the very word Chardonnay. If that's you I'm talking about, you're missing one of the great white wine pleasures. This Chardonnay from the cool maritime Mornington Peninsula, south of Melbourne, will convince you. There's nothing coarse or brash about this, simply a gorgeous flavour of fresh brioche and hazelnut, oatmeal and apple and peach. But the flavours by themselves are less important than the texture, the balance, the weight and length, the sheer pleasure and drinkability.

9   2004 Rioja, Amenital, Bodegas Miguel Ángel Muro, Spain, 14% abv
Big Red Wine Company, £15

2004 is a classic vintage for Rioja: dark, ripe, rather closed in, promising long life. Well, this is dark, but it isn't brooding and introspective. The fruit's darkness is the darkness of real ripeness, so ripe that a heady plum blossom scent shimmers on the surface of the wine. It does have some tannic toughness, but not nearly enough to interfere with the pleasure, and it's the fruit acidity that provides the backbone to the wine. You don't usually get that tingling acidity in modern Rioja, but here they've used 20% of the Graciano grape in the blend (along with the traditional Tempranillo) to provide vivacity and verve. The acidity keeps the wine fresh while the waxy texture and mellow vanilla warmth wrap around the fruit and ooze over your palate.

10   2007 Cabernet Sauvignon, Ringbolt, Margaret River, Western Australia, 14.5% abv
Tesco, £8.99; also at Cambridge Wine Merchants, Flagship Wines, Nidderdale Fine Wines

People often say that the Margaret River, in Western Australia, has conditions that closely mirror those of Bordeaux in France. Well, both regions are close to the sea, but Bordeaux should be so lucky as to produce red wines like this at a price like this. OK, it is quite Bordeaux-like in texture – somewhere between warm summer earth and shiny smooth pebbles – and this provides an appetizing, rather savoury background to the piercing blackcurrant fruit, lightly tinged with blackcurrant leaf, graphite and mint.

11 **2006 Cabernet-Malbec, Tim Adams, Clare Valley, South Australia, 14.5% abv**

AustralianWineCentre.co.uk, £12

Malbec isn't a grape the Australians pay much attention to – except in the Clare Valley, where it has a long and honourable pedigree. Tim Adams has crafted a wine both powerful and beautiful – dense yet scented Cabernet blackcurrant and black plum cosying up to Malbec damson skins, and both of these luxuriating in the mild toastiness of brioche as well as feeling the grainy dryness of stones and bleached herbs. And over everything floats a kind of blue haze of autumn-ripened fruit.

12 **2009 Sauvignon Blanc, Clifford Bay, Villa Maria, Marlborough, New Zealand, 13.5% abv**

Oddbins, Sainsbury's, £13.49

New Zealand Sauvignon should be tangy, green, tingling, dry – but an increasing amount of Kiwi Sauvignon is tasting wishy-washy, sometimes sweaty, sugary and soft. Thank goodness for Clifford Bay. The vines are towards the windy, chilly seashore at the far edge of Marlborough. You can taste the wind and the sea spray in this wine; everything is tangy and appetizing – nettles, horseradish, green apples, tomato leaf and even English mustard – everything savoury or green, yet the wine is ripe and full in the mouth and there's even a slight chewiness, like grape skin or tomato skin, to titillate your tongue.

13 2008 Blanc de Morgex et de La Salle, 'Rayon', La Cave du Vin Blanc de Morgex et de La Salle, Valle d'Aosta, Italy, 12.5% abv

♀ Les Caves de Pyrène, £12.99

You almost need to wear ski-gloves and a bobble hat to drink this: it's grown high up in the Alpine passes on the French-Italian border. You can taste the icy tumbling streams flinging themselves against the gaunt rock face as the waters cascade towards the lazy freedom of the north Italian plains, but that chill minerality is marvellously complemented by a deliciously ripe apple fruit, mixed citrus peel and a positively lush yet dry texture of wax and rock dust.

14 2008 Riesling, Bassermann-Jordan, Pfalz, Germany, 10% abv

♀ Waitrose, £8.99

They used to call them the '3 Bs' – Bürklin-Wolf, von Buhl and Bassermann-Jordan – and they totally dominated quality winemaking in Germany's Rheinpfalz region. But new generations arrived, new ideas too, and the '3 Bs' seemed increasingly out of touch and old-fashioned. But at last they've woken up to the 21st century and are once again setting the pace from their superbly sited vineyard slopes. This is absurdly easy to drink. It's clean, bright, mouthwatering, with cool, clearwater stones and a spritzy prickle nipping at your tongue, while an irresistible fruit salad of Cox's apple, white peach, raisins and runny honey bathes your palate in delight.

• Waitrose also sell a fabulous, lighter Dr Wagner Riesling (£7.99) from the Mosel.

15 2005 Priorat, Coma Vella, Mas d'en Gil, Catalunya, Spain, 15% abv
♥ Waitrose, £22.99

Old vineyards, modern equipment and winemaking – that's often a potent combination for fine wine. These vines average 50 years old and marry the old traditional varieties of Cariñena, Garnacha Peluda and Garnacha País with the new-wave interlopers of Cabernet and Syrah. This has reduced the old-style shrivelled date and raisin Priorat flavour and replaced it with something more exciting and, if anything, denser but more focused; a darkness like ink and iodine rages with black plum and black cherry syrup; licorice drapes itself around the taste; even the stony structure is black and wild and barely under control.

16 2005 Douro, La Rosa Reserve, Quinta de la Rosa, Portugal, 14% abv
♥ Oxford Wine Company, £26.95

This is ambitious wine. La Rosa already make excellent port and a beautifully balanced, fragrant dry Douro red: fragrance and balance, elegance almost, have made La Rosa's reputation. Then they decide to kick all

their restraint into the long grass and go for the monster. Remarkably they've created a beautiful beast rather than an ogre, and the fundamental joy of La Rosa remains intact despite some pretty gaudy trappings. This wine is genuinely big and powerful, genuinely oaky too, but the oak doesn't stifle the fruit and the aroma: orchard-ripe blackberry and damson cavort with marzipan solemnity and maypole floral scent. Or is maypole too bright and breezy? Perhaps the scent is more the sultry violets and drooping blossoms of a hidden bower in humid summer sun.

17 2008 Riesling, Tim Adams, Clare Valley, South Australia, 11.5% abv
♀ Tesco, £9.29

One of the great bargains of the wine scene. World-class Riesling for less than a tenner. It is strange how we're still so unwilling to give Riesling the plaudits it deserves – but try it once, and you're certain to go back again. Just sip this fabulous citrus zesty liquid, boiled lemon and apple peel, a whole coil of Granny Smith peel, pith and zest and chalk, and then leather and aniseed and shortbread dough.

18 2006 Ribera del Duero Crianza, Viña Pedrosa, Bodegas Pérez Pascuas, Castilla y León, Spain, 14% abv
♟ Bancroft Wines, £24.95

Ribera del Duero has become such a soaring success in recent years that prices have gone bonkers. This one, from Pedrosa, is a triumphant wine that sort of justifies its price tag by sheer force of personality. It is oaky – great wafts of vanilla, cream and hazelnut drape themselves around the wine – and it's difficult to say precisely what the fruit actually is – it's dark, almost black, but what is it? Actually, it doesn't matter, because you suddenly realize the fruit and tannin and oak have melded together in your mouth into a rich, balanced, rather awesome whole which makes extra description superfluous.

19 2009 Polena, Donnafugata, Sicily, Italy, 12.5% abv
♀ Oddbins, £14.49; Valvona & Crolla, £11.95

The new wave of Italian whites gets better every year, and the choice for those who are tired of oaky Chardonnay or zesty Sauvignon grows ever wider. You get zest here – a thrilling Sicilian lemon mix of pith and peel and scent from the Catarratto grape that mingles with the dry blossomy perfume of Viognier and joins forces with mountain herbs freshness and the graininess of apricot skin to cut through the fat juiciness of apricot flesh and spice. Freshness and scent, chubbiness cut through with zest, green yet lush; really good modern white.

20 2007 Small Berry Mourvèdre, Cline, Contra Costa County, California, USA, 15% abv
🍷 Oddbins, £24.99; also at The Wine Treasury

I remember this vineyard. James May and I drove out there because I wanted to show him what might be the oldest vines in California. I was thrilled to find this little patch of history nestling among the eucalyptus trees barely 100 yards from the San Joaquin River. The sandy soil has kept these vines disease-free since the 19th century. You can smell those eucalyptus trees in the wine – and I love that exotic resiny fragrance that bounces back and forth between spearmint leaf freshness, lovage and savory and lime zest depending on which bit of your palate the wine hits first. And this scent is important in such a rich, soft wine – those ancient vines give small, concentrated amounts of intense black fruit – blackcurrant and blackberry, morello cherry and damson, as well as a hint of rustic 'aroma', all creating really interesting, primordial stuff.

21 2009 Torrontes, Nómade, Cafayate, Salta, Argentina, 13.5% abv
♀ Armit, £10.25

I suppose 'nomad' isn't a bad name for a wine if the label says that the producer 'personally walks every inch of the Los Andes area'. Quite a big area, those Andes. At least, with all his tramping about, he found a good, high-altitude vineyard site for the fragrant Torrontes grape, because this is a grape that can easily become oily and flat in excessive heat, but high in the Andes can produce thrilling flavours, serious yet heady and exotic at the same time. This has a memorable violet and tea rose aroma and a flavour that is weighty but awash with a magic potion of leather and violet and grapefruit, lime and lemon marmalade.

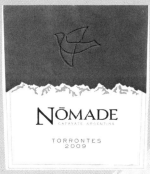

22 2001 Rioja Reserva, Viña Arana, La Rioja Alta, Spain, 13% abv
♟ Armit, Tanners, Waitrose, £19.99

Ah, this brings back memories. Arana is an old-fashioned style from the excellent
Rioja Alta company and 2001 is a classic year, but I still didn't expect quite such an
old-time classic as this. Its hue is well past the first flush of youth, but the flavour is
simply divine. Dry, sure, even a little faded, but only in the way a great beauty may
fade into something less arresting, more demure. The fruit is no longer crisp and
bouncy – in fact it's faintly squashy and bruised, like end-of-season strawberries,
bletted medlars, plums and rosehips and tinned golden peaches. Wrap all this in
mellow hazelnut and crème fraîche oak and you're in for a treat from another era.

23 2007 Cabernet Sauvignon, Robert Mondavi Winery, Napa Valley, USA, 15.5% abv
♟ Majestic, £19.99

There was a time when Robert Mondavi bestrode California's wine world, pint-sized but imperial. He died in
2008 and it seems fitting to me that this wine – the last vintage he saw – is the best I can remember for a
long time. A ripe, classic Napa wine, rich, scented with morello cherry and blackcurrant, with a broad
confident texture oozing black fruit and the graininess of marzipan splashed with kirsch. I'd keep it for a few
years yet, and then drink it, in valedictory mood, to the great man's memory.

24 2007 Mencía, Gaba do Xil, Telmo Rodríguez, Valdeorras,
Spain, 13% abv
♟ Adnams, £8.99

Valdeorras and its Mencía grape variety are starting to make waves now,
but they were little regarded until Telmo Rodríguez and his peers arrived to

explore. Now people are talking about a new Spanish classic. This is deep and dark, and though it smells a bit meaty, the flavour is all dense, rich fruit, blackberry and black cherry, made exciting and unusual by a lick of fish oil and the sappiness of springtime wood bark and rounded off by cocoa dust.

25 2007 Puligny-Montrachet, Les Corvées des Vignes, Domaine Maroslavac-Leger, Burgundy, France, 13% abv
♀ Goedhuis, £24.97

It sounds strange to say that this is a bit of a bargain, but top white Burgundy is in very short supply and Puligny is the greatest of the white wine villages there. This is pure, limpid, absolutely classic Puligny. A zingy acidity runs like an electric current through it, complementing the oatmeal and hazelnut richness which, with time, will get a mellow chocolatey veneer to go with the glittering minerality that shines like tiny particles of quartz in the heart of the wine.

26 2008 Empordá, Sauló, Espelt, Catalunya, Spain, 14% abv
♀ Oxford Wine Company, £12.49

Empordá is the hinterland behind the Costa Brava resorts. I've been going there for years, tasting the wines dutifully but without joy, and I'd rather decided that all the locally-trumpeted quality I kept hearing about was probably just home team shouting. But on my last visit I tasted some rather good fresh young *joven* reds, and now this arrives. It's a serious, weighty red, but, in an era of excess, remarkable for its restraint. The flavour of rich strawberry coulis mashed up with red cherries is almost syrupy in its concentration, yet is dry and reserved, perfumed with bay leaf and thyme and mineral dust: sweet and rich, yet fresh and appetizingly dry.

27 2006 Semillon, The Willows, Barossa Valley, South Australia, 12.5% abv

♀ AustralianWineCentre.co.uk, £11

The Willows is a pleasure factory, pure and simple. Reds or whites, it doesn't matter, they amiably go on doling out pleasure by the bucketload. This is fabulous stuff, effortlessly knitting together the opposing flavours of lemon juice, grapefruit pith and zest and coffee beans with hazel and cashew nut warmth. It manages to be rich yet austere at the same time, and will get ever mellower with age.

28 2008 Chablis, Daniel Dampt & Fils, Burgundy, France, 12.5% abv

♀ Haynes Hanson & Clark, £13.10

Daniel Dampt is one of Chablis' most consistent performers and this is proper Chablis, not mucked about with, not over-oaked or over-ripened or over-alcoholized. The wine is mostly about minerality and reserve – smelling of damp, clean stones drying in a springtime breeze, of lemon zest and juice, a drop or two of apple syrup and a smear of honey, and just a hint of unnerving pheromonal scent. The palate is stony, steely to start with, but opens out into a mellowness almost nut sweet, almost as creamy and scented as oatmeal.

29 2009 Vinho Verde Tinto, Afros Vinhão, Portugal, 12.5% abv

♟ Les Caves de Pyrène, £12.49

Dark purple, seemingly ultra-ripe and bubbling over with black cherry and rosa plum scent that is brutally shoved aside by gum-challenging sourness and a distinct whiff of the farmyard; dense plum and strawberry fruit gives way to tobacco and the chewy torture of underripe damson skins; back comes Christmas cake spice and raisins to be washed away in a flood of grainy skins and apple peel. Wild or what? And I love it.

30 2007 Ribera del Duero, Psi, Dominio de Pingus, Castilla y León, Spain, 13.5% abv

🍷 Corney & Barrow, £22.99

Pingus is a superstar red wine that attracts hysterical interest for its tiny production of stratospherically-priced nectar. Psi is its baby brother; it's still expensive – but, hey, check out the price of the full banana. Baby bro, but giving you a pretty good idea of what Pingus is all about. Fabulous texture for a start. This wine has a lively tannin and is quite oaky, but the texture of fruit and spice is the main event. The fruit is ultra-red rather than black – powerful lush red cherry and red plum – with a really bright scent that easily handles the rasp of herbs and sinks contentedly into the soft doughy embrace of cherry cake.

31 2006 Cabernet Sauvignon, The Willows, Barossa Valley, South Australia, 14.5% abv

🍷 AustralianWineCentre.co.uk, £15

A sybaritic cavalcade of rich, ripe fruit and spice. Eucalyptus oil and mint, sweet blackcurrant, morello cherries and chocolate – but it's bitter black chocolate and the treacle it's draped in is black. So this isn't just deep red lollipop juice, it's serious wine and it'll get even better with age, but the seriousness never gets in the way of putting a big smile on your purple-stained lips.

32 2008 Sauvignon Blanc, Cape Crest, Te Mata, Hawkes Bay, New Zealand, 13% abv

♀ Majestic, £17.49

Te Mata is famous for Cabernet-based reds and an inspired Chardonnay, Elston. But I've tasted their barrel-fermented Sauvignon regularly over the years and, after a slow start, it's really singing nowadays. The Sauvignon bursts forth with

good grapefruit zestiness and green apple crispness, but the effect of barrel fermentation shows in a scented nectarine richness and the soft creaminess of custard.

33 2006 Cabernet Sauvignon-Cabernet Franc-Petit Verdot, Sanguine Estate, Heathcote, Victoria, Australia, 15.5% abv
❦ Great Western Wine, £14.40

Heathcote has very quickly made itself a stellar reputation for smooth, unctuous Shiraz grown on its 510 million-year-old traffic-light red soils. But Shiraz is not the only grape in town. This is a blend of three Bordeaux varieties, not quite as swish as the Shiraz, but still a really good drop, which will be greatly softened and sweetened if you open it for an hour or two before you drink it. The flavours do have some of the austere grandeur of top Bordeaux, but the Aussie ripe fruit eagerness to please won't go away. Graphite, coal dust and grainy tannin are there, but not nearly so evidently as purple-ripe plums, cleansing acidity and spice, and soft enveloping toffee cream.

34 2009 Cheverny, Clos du Tue-Boeuf, Loire Valley, France, 12% abv
❦ Les Caves de Pyrène, Oddbins, £14.99

I've always thought of Cheverny as white wine country, one of the little eddies of the Loire Valley, clinging on precariously to a wine existence on the fringes. Clearly global warming is being kind to the Loire if areas like

Cheverny can produce gorgeous, juicy reds like this. In fact, the ability to only just ripen the red grapes is what gives this wine its ridiculously drinkable appeal: it combines both red and white wine flavours with a smack of minerality. This is a riot of floral scent, red cherry and strawberry fruit jumbled delightfully together with pink apples and rosehips, goldengage and quince. With a rub of wax and a sprinkling of graphite, it's a truly original exuberant red.

35   2005 Saint-Joseph Les Coteaux, Eric & Joel Durand, Rhône Valley, France, 13% abv
🍷 Great Western Wine, £18.55

St-Joseph is a wine that positively benefits from five to ten years' aging, but which we usually drink at a mere two or three years old. So it's a joy to find one hitting five years old. This is deliciously ripe, full of ripe black plum and raspberry fruit, coated in dusty black chocolate cream, yet tempered by a refreshing seasoning of pepper, celery and graphite.

36   2008 Malbec, Loma Larga, Casablanca Valley, Chile, 14.5% abv
🍷 Justerini and Brooks, £12.26

I think of Malbec as Argentina's signature grape nowadays, but Chile's having a go too. Rather than planting Malbec in warm conditions similar to Argentina's Mendoza, this one's from the decidedly cool Casablanca Valley. It's as dark and purple as any Argentine version, and the fruit is sweet and fat, but it isn't so lush, so chubby. Instead the sweetness is blackcurrant and plum, sharpened and refined by acidity, made chewy with licorice and plum skins – and it finishes with a reassuring smear of smoky chocolate.

37   2007 Syrah, Montes Alpha, Colchagua Valley, Chile, 14% abv
🍷 Waitrose, £11.49

Montes have always sought a dark, brooding style because their magnificent Apalta mountain slope vineyards give very dark, brooding fruit. Recently they've developed new vineyards at Marchígue, nearer the coast, and the fruit is much more scented and come-hither, and makes an ideal partner for old beetle-brow from Apalta. This is the softest Alpha Syrah yet, but is quite profound enough for me, with its ripe plum, cherry, loganberry and blackberry fruit, and its serious structured texture.

38 2008 Soave Classico, Monte Fiorentine, Ca'Rugate, Veneto, Italy, 12.5% abv

Bancroft Wines, £14.95

Soave's getting really good nowadays. I'm talking top end Soave here, but even basic cheap Soave is unrecognizable from the lifeless baked rubbish they used to churn out barely a decade ago. Most Soaves are blends of grapes, but this is 100% Garganega – a lovely, waxy, scented grape. This is scented all right – smelling like last year's pot-pourri, dried rose petals and slightly bruised apple purée. Soft, succulent, with surprisingly good acidity nipping at waxy texture and pink apple flesh fruit. Good Soave has the rare ability to be soft and lush, yet fresh and appetizing – you'd think the wines can't be serious and ageworthy, but they are.

39 2007 Chardonnay, The Olive Grove, d'Arenberg, McLaren Vale-Adelaide Hills, South Australia, 14% abv

Bibendum, Oddbins, Sainsbury's, £8.99

Not too much modern about this, but as an old-style bushwhacker, it's spot on. In fact, that's not quite fair. I suspect in the old days this would have been 100% from the hot McLaren Vale, whereas here they've blended in 45% of fruit from the cooler Adelaide Hills. That allows the wine to be big and rich, almost chewy and a bit funky – yet with surprising acidity, hazelnut softness and just a dab of honey.

40 2008 Minervois La Livinière, Domaine des Garennes, Gérard Bertrand, Languedoc-Roussillon, France, 14.5% abv

Marks & Spencer, £10.49

Minervois is one of southern France's best zones for red wines, famed for its ability to create scented reds in conditions that really should be too hot for scent to survive. Gérard Bertrand is a past master at drawing the best out of the south's different conditions and he's crafted a rich, juicy wine, full of all the black fruits – damson, cherry, blackberry – scorched a tiny bit by the sun as the hint of hot stone and dates shows, but above all delightfully scented with jasmine and violet.

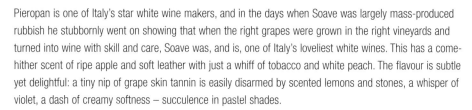

41   2009 Soave, Pieropan, Veneto, Italy, 12% abv
♀ Booths, Colchester Wine Co, Lea & Sandeman, Liberty Wines, WoodWinters, £11.99–£12.99

Pieropan is one of Italy's star white wine makers, and in the days when Soave was largely mass-produced rubbish he stubbornly went on showing that when the right grapes were grown in the right vineyards and turned into wine with skill and care, Soave was, and is, one of Italy's loveliest white wines. This has a come-hither scent of ripe apple and soft leather with just a whiff of tobacco and white peach. The flavour is subtle yet delightful: a tiny nip of grape skin tannin is easily disarmed by scented lemons and stones, a whisper of violet, a dash of creamy softness – succulence in pastel shades.

42   2008 Riesling Smaragd, Kaiserberg, Prager, Wachau, Austria, 13% abv
♀ Waitrose, £25.99

Riesling is a transparent grape variety, one where the flavours of the vineyard shine like beams of starlight through the wine. Well, this Riesling comes from impossibly steep vineyards of virtually pure rock, teetering above the river Danube, and you can taste the tension, the risk and the rock in the wine. Aggressive acidity and stones rage against each other and will do for years yet, but this mineral pungency is soothed by a slowly fattening, mellow honey and yeasty cream that cajoles the steep slope arrogance without ever quite extinguishing it.

43   2007 Pinot Noir, Palliser Estate, Martinborough, New Zealand, 14% abv

🍷 Justerini and Brooks, £14.71; Virgin £14.99

Palliser Pinot Noir was one of the first New Zealand reds to make any kind of impression over here, back in the 1990s. Pinot Noir has since proven that its reputation for being a difficult grape was at least partly a Burgundian smokescreen, and New Zealand has now developed half a dozen places where Pinot Noir produces wines of clearly defined personalities. So savour a glass of this ripe, smooth red. Its plum and blackberry sweetness is roughened slightly by grainy tannin, its well-behaved perfume deliciously perverted by an aroma of undergrowth and the sizzling, spitting, fatty smoke of a beefsteak on the barbie.

44   2008 Veltliner, Eisacktal, Peter Pliger, Alto Adige, Italy, 14% abv

🍷 Les Caves de Pyrène, £17.99

This is the Grüner Veltliner grape, which makes such striking, rocky, savoury wines along the rugged banks of the Danube in Austria. The grape clearly relishes the difficult life: these vineyards are high in the Dolomite mountains. Cold, yes, but also mountain-sunny – a great combination for dry, aromatic white wines. The Veltliner is usually marked by savoury flavours along with the fruit, and this is full and ripe, almost gentle, with a savouriness as creamy as avocado, as mild as petits pois, a scent matching meatiness with mountain flowers and a remarkably fresh richness of marzipan splashed with sweet Cox's apple juice.

45   2007 Amarone della Valpolicella (Cantina Valpantena), Veneto, Italy, 14.5% abv

🍷 Sainsbury's Taste the Difference, £14.99

The last few years have seen British supermarkets one by one reveal really good examples of Amarone, one of Italy's greatest traditional red wine styles. And they're affordable: OK, it *is* a lot of money, but it's a damn sight less than fine Amarone normally is. Amarone is supposed to have a kind of bitter-rich quality, which intensifies with age. Before being made into wine, the grapes are placed on wooden trays to dry for three months, and if some of them virtually turn to dates in the meantime and others begin to tire and fade on the trays – that's all part of the wine's personality. This one is more rich than bitter – though the balance might change with a few years' aging – and there is some surprisingly fresh loganberry fruit and burnished mineral scent to go with the black chocolate and the whisper of decay from those months spent drying.

46   2009 Sauvignon Blanc, Vin de Pays d'Oc, Averys Project Winemaker, Languedoc, France, 12.5% abv
♀ Averys, £7.99

I didn't expect to be putting a Sauvignon from southern France into my top 100, but this isn't any old southern French Sauvignon – the core of the fruit comes from the cool, high, limestone vineyards of Limoux, famous for snappy Blanquette de Limoux fizz. And it's been fermented and aged very skilfully in oak barrels. There's a green leafy scent, joined by apple blossom and Comice pear skin, and these scents linger on in the flavour and mingle with soft, creamy oak and the crisp orchard sweetness of nectarines.

47   2009 Côte Roannaise, Les Vieilles Vignes, Domaine Robert Sérol, Loire Valley, France, 12% abv
♀ Christopher Piper Wines, £8.85

This mouthwatering red is made from Gamay, the same grape as Beaujolais – but no one outside France has ever heard of it. That's because it's hidden in the hills behind Beaujolais and it got left out of the appellation and missed all the razzmatazz which briefly made Beaujolais rich and famous. So there was nothing for it but to continue making really excellent red gluggers, more brawny than Beaujolais – but it's a fabulous brawn built on graphite and sun-warmed river rocks, and also richer – a superripe mix of stewed peaches and strawberries, sprayed with tree sap and promising chocolate and cream with a year or two's age.

48   2008 Tempranillo, Clare Hills, Pikes Vintners, Clare Valley, South Australia, 14% abv
Laithwaites, £9.49

They love challenges up in the Clare Valley. So when a new grape – for Australia – like Tempranillo comes along, you can be sure that the Clare growers will be at the head of the queue for vine cuttings to plant. Each Clare Tempranillo I've had so far has been lovely, and here's another. It's really drinkable, really original, blending eucalyptus and lime zest with rosehips and squashy strawberries; not dense, just beautifully balanced – in fact it's lighter and more fragrant than a typical Spanish Tempranillo and yet has more flavour.

49   2005 Côtes de Bergerac, Château Montdoyen, South-West France, 14.5% abv
Great Western Wine, £10.95

2005 is a stellar year for Bordeaux, which is just down the road from Bergerac. This could be a really classy Bordeaux 2005. Except for one thing. It would cost two or three times as much. This is dense and ripe, brooding and serious, hinting at a little scent, but keen to sport mineral strength and dark, long-haul, complex fruit. It's pretty closed and concentrated just now – I'd keep it for three to five years – but if you wanted the great 2005 red Bordeaux and couldn't afford them, treat yourself to some of this.

50   2009 Sauvignon Blanc, Cederberg, South Africa, 13% abv
♀ Bancroft Wines, £11.95, Stone, Vine & Sun, £10.75

South Africa has recently been making itself a reputation for really tangy Sauvignons. Most of these come from windswept coastal vineyards where you can taste the brine and the bracing gales. But Cederberg has chosen a different route to achieve the sunny yet cool conditions that produce great Sauvignon – it has the highest vineyards in South Africa, and the higher you get, the cooler you get. This is almost spritzy-fresh – zesty, tangy, snapping with the palate-slapping flavours of green apple, peppercorn and lemon zest, scented with summer dust and softened by the demure sweetness of green figs.

51   2007 Syrah, Vidal, Hawkes Bay, New Zealand, 14% abv
♥ Flagship Wines, Halifax Wine Co, New Zealand House of Wine, Waitrose, Wimbledon Wine Cellar, £10.99

Vidal was one of the first New Zealand Syrahs I tasted at the beginning of the century and its world-changing flavours send shivers of excitement through my winetasting memory. There had never been a Syrah like those Hawkes Bay Syrahs of less than 10 years ago. So pure, so soft, yet so fresh and crisp, somehow seamlessly marrying ripe blackberry with the snap of a celery stick and the lazy, drifting scent of lilies. Vidal is still excellent, and is one of the most affordable. It doesn't offer you lily scent, but it has fascinating ripe redcurrant, raspberry and cherry fruit, it's seasoned with lovage, white pepper and celery, dusted with mild cocoa powder, and it flows down your throat hardly touching the sides.

52 2007 Malbec Reserva, Jean Bousquet, Tupungato Valley, Mendoza, Argentina, 14.5% abv
♥ Vintage Roots, £10.99

Malbec is by nature a scented grape, lush in texture, chubby and charming. But it can have the charm literally baked out of it by relentless sun. That's why the best Argentine Malbecs are grown at over 1000 metres altitude: as you go higher up the Andean valleys you get cooler vineyards and wines of increasing scent and focused fruit. Tupungato is Mendoza's highest point and this explains the scented succulence of this wine – a gentle violet and sweet leather perfume, ripe, fresh, orchard-scented damson fruit and just a nip of plum skins bitterness to stop you giggling with delight as you drink it.

53 2004 Shiraz, Ebenezer, Barossa Valley Estate, Barossa Valley, South Australia, 14.5% abv
♥ Nidderdale Fine Wines, £19.50

Ebenezer is one of the famous traditional Barossa Shirazes. Some of its peers have got so obsessed with their own importance in recent years that the over-alcoholic, over-extracted oak soup that appears under their labels is undrinkable – and wildly expensive. But not Ebenezer. This is positively mouthwatering – not an adjective I'd normally use for a Barossa Shiraz. It's big, sure – packed with black chocolate and licorice – but it's also beautifully balanced by acidity so that the stewed plum fruit can lurch indulgently towards a smoky, syrupy richness, but it never loses its freshness and ability to please.

54 2008 Syrah, Costero, Viña Leyda, Leyda Valley, Chile, 14% abv
♥ Majestic, £8.99

Leyda is one of Chile's newest, coolest, sea-influenced wine areas. It shot to prominence a few years ago with brilliantly tangy Sauvignon, and followed this up with fresh, vibrant Pinot Noir – and now it's Syrah's turn. Predictably, it's fantastic: dark, crunchy, crisp, scented; it even has a little lily in its perfume, but the heart of the wine is shovels full of black pepper and stewed black plums fruit, pepper, celery and savoury lovage bite, wrapped in rich but nicely bitter-edged black chocolate.

55 2007 Chardonnay, Opou Vineyard, Millton, Gisborne, New Zealand, 14% abv
♀ Vintage Roots, £11.75

Gisborne is one of the rainier, more humid parts of New Zealand's vinescape, so you'd expect to have to spray against rot and disease, yet the leading Kiwi organic and biodynamic producer James Millton says the humidity and the fertile soils provide conditions so full of the forces needed for life that they strengthen, not weaken, the vine. I visited this year and was hooked. Here's an example of what James does: delightfully gentle, seductive Chardonnay with the soft texture of Victoria sponge cake and confectioners' cream, a mellow flavour of scented oatmeal, hazelnut and Mum's rice pudding and a self-effacing lemony acidity.

56 2008 Chenin, Touraine Azay-le-Rideau, Pascal Pibaleau, Loire Valley, France, 13.3% abv
♀ Christopher Piper Wines, £8.50

Most of the whites that we see from Touraine are tasty Sauvignons, but the Chenin Blanc gives wines of enormous character there too. This organic number has a heavenly kitchen smell like tarte Tatin – ripe cooking apples, buttery syrup just slightly burnt, and gooey pastry. But it's not sweet, just beautifully rich with a kind of ripe, sour fruit, a stony and dried herbs rasp and fruit syrup cut with good acidity.

57 2008 Vermentino, Lunae, Colli di Luni, Lunae Bosoni, Liguria, Italy, 13% abv
♀ Armit, £12.99

We just about never see Ligurian wines in the UK. When you look at the tiny slivers of land among the mountain slopes tumbling down to the Mediterranean that make up the region, I'm surprised we see any. But both reds and whites are really characterful and this is an oddball delight, a fascinating mix of waxy weight, boudoir scent and freshness. The flavour is a gorgeous paradox, teetering between a pumice stone dryness you can almost lick, and a lush fatness half Oil of Olay, half Neutrogena glycerine soap (that's enough product placement: ed). This may sound as though it's got gobs of flavour, but in typical Italian white style, the wine coats your mouth with texture and suggests, rather than parades, its irresistibly surprising blend of flavours.

58   2008 Malbec, Achaval Ferrer, Mendoza, Argentina, 14% abv
♥ Corney & Barrow, £13.99

Classic Argentine Malbec. In fact classic Malbec, with the textbook flavours of leather and fish oil skirting the lush heart of black plum and damson flesh made richer with black chocolate, but kept refreshing and bright with the rub of stones and the chewy nip of damson skin.

59   2008 Riesling, Mountadam, Eden Valley, South Australia, 13% abv
♀ Justerini and Brooks, £10.80

Eden Valley, in the hills behind the more famous Barossa Valley, is, along with the Clare Valley, the heart of South Australian Riesling. Clare is usually leaner, Eden more scented; this wine catches a bit of both styles, being ripe and slightly plump – for a Riesling – yet cut through with grapefruit and lemon zest tang and just a hint of that fascinating toasty flavour Aussie Rieslings develop as they mature.

60   2008 Douro Reserva, Quinta de la Rosa/Waitrose, Portugal, 13.5% abv
♥ Waitrose, £9.99

Quinta de la Rosa was one of the first Douro properties to realize that you could make great red table wine in the Douro Valley, not just sweet fortified port, and since they made a gentle scented port, they decided to make a gentle scented dry red. Well, it's not all that gentle – it's big, serious and dark – but it does have a heavenly scent of jasmine and violets that mingles with graphite and blackcurrant leaf and runs right through the wine. Lush deep raspberry and loganberry fruit is kept in check by the cool rub of tannin, and not overwhelmed with vanilla oak.

61 2009 Gros Manseng, Selection, Côtes de Gascogne, Domaine des Cassagnoles, South-West France, 13.5% abv

♀ Christopher Piper Wines, £6.80

Wine doesn't have to be expensive to get into the top 100, it just has to be a damned good drink. And this is a smasher. It comes from the Côtes de Gascogne – where much of France's best-value white comes from – but, unusually, it's from a single estate and it's had some barrel fermentation. This produces a fabulous lemon meringue pie melange of soft and sharp: grapefruit, nectarine and apple flesh fruit, grated lemon zest and mint leaf freshness and a delightful softness halfway between spiced custard and citrus meringue.

62 2008 Pinot Noir, Paper Road, Borthwick Vineyard, Wairarapa, New Zealand, 13.5% abv

♟ Armit, £12.35

Borthwick is part of a new wave of Pinot makers in New Zealand, who are developing land a little way outside the initial plantings. These plantings are quickly proving their worth. This is serious Pinot: waxy, glyceriny in texture, with dark cherry and plum jam fruit softened by toffee and roughened up by a good scrape of fresh earth.

63 2009 Vinho Verde, Quinta de Azevedo, Sogrape, Portugal, 11% abv

♀ Majestic, £6.24; Stevens Garnier, £6.95; Waitrose, £6.69

This was quite simply one of the most thirst-quenching, utterly enjoyable white wines of the summer. Frankly, with wine as mouthwatering as this, as low in alcohol and as tantalizingly dry, who needs expensive Sauvignon? Well, I wouldn't give up my Sauvignons, but this is a great replacement – yet it's totally different in flavour. It comes from Portugal's wet, squally north. You can smell the sea and the seaweed, you can taste the summer showers and the brief bursts of sun before the Atlantic gales return. Lemons, green apples, peach blossom, all rainwashed, then a magic flavour of sweet white peach, Comice pear flesh and almonds, scrubbed with pumice, dragged across pebbles, sprayed with brine. All this and a teasing spritzy prickle on your tongue.

64   2006 Amarone della Valpolicella, Rocca Alata (Cantina di Soave), Veneto, Italy, 14.5% abv
🍷 Tesco Finest, £14.99

Good, powerful stuff: lots of the black chocolate bitterness you expect from Amarone, powerful sweet fruit, but also a very appetizing Italian hint of sourness as though someone had splashed a little balsamic vinegar into the vat. But the heart of the wine is a syrup-rich wallop of black cherry, plum and blackberry, softened a little by cake dough and kept serious with a hefty slug of that black chocolate bitterness.

65   2008 Sangiovese, Vat 12, Deen De Bortoli, King Valley, Victoria, Australia, 13.5% abv
🍷 Oddbins, £10.99

Sangiovese is the grape that makes Italy's Chianti; it isn't easy to make into easy-drinking wine, but this is an excellent example by any standards, with a typical ripe tomato, cherry and strawberry fruitiness mixing it with rocky, grainy tannin, decent acidity and a handful of dried herbs.

66 **2007 Côtes du Roussillon-Villages, Bila-Haut, M. Chapoutier, Roussillon, France, 14% abv**
Booths, £6.99

Chapoutier's fame lies with its Rhône Valley wines, but it's expanding its operations both in France and overseas. Roussillon is right down on the Spanish border. It's hot, windy and arid and Chapoutier has tamed these conditions without enfeebling the wine. The fruit is big and red and wind-dried – dried cherry and cranberry and plum – with a swish of sun-bleached herbs and a touch of licorice blackness that opens out at the last moment into a full, almost rich, raspberry finish.

67 **2008 Pinot Gris, Cave de Turckheim, Alsace, France, 13% abv**
Tesco Finest, £6.99

Pinot Gris – in its Italian manifestation Pinot Grigio – has come to mean a glass of something inoffensive and forgettable. Well, here's what Pinot Gris – in its French manifestation – should really taste like. This is bursting with character and flavour, piling up rough, earthy honey and leather with window putty and peach stones and that cat's tongue furriness of peach skins, and wrapping it in a sensual pheromonal coat of cream. Not a white for the faint-hearted, but absolutely what real, self-confident Pinot Gris should be.

68 **2004 Semillon, Margaret, Peter Lehmann, Barossa, South Australia, 11.5% abv**
Vin du Van, £14.50

Peter Lehmann is one of the heroes of Australian wine and he's still a big enough softie to name a wine after his beloved wife, bless him. Well, it's a corker: classic Aussie Semillon which you're going to love or loathe. I love it. Still young at 6½ years old, still green-tinted gold, and yet mature flavours are starting to wrestle with the youth. Apple acid and citrus oil austerity keep the wine in shape, as a more rumpled punchbowl of strawberry custard and pith and a nuttiness that's got a kind of 'sweaty, don't wash a lot, but jeez I'm a charmer' larrikin grin starts to muscle in. If I tell you my final note was that the wine gave 'the promise of soft, creamy home bosom' – does that help explain what it's like? Or maybe that's why Peter named it after his wife.

69 2008 Shiraz-Viognier, Bloodstone, Gemtree Vineyards, McLaren Vale, South Australia, 14.5% abv
🍷 Vin du Van, £10.50

2008 was a very hot summer in McLaren Vale, just south of Adelaide. Some black grapes were coming into the winery with a potential alcoholic strength of 21%. It was really difficult to keep any freshness in the wines, but one way was to blend a little white Viognier into the red Shiraz. That means the deep chocolate and blackberry fruit gets a lift from a little floral scent and some soft sweet peach flesh. It works, but the wine is always going to be very much on the rich, ripe side.

70 2006 Shiraz, Patchwork, Yalumba, Barossa Valley, South Australia, 14.5% abv
🍷 Flagship Wines, £11.25; Laithwaites, £11.49; Nidderdale Fine Wines, £11.99

This is exactly what people expect when they buy a Barossa Shiraz. It's a rich, true-to-form old style of wine, mixing dates and prunes with chocolate and black treacle, chunky and dense, but still fresh and appetizing, never overbearing, just a damned good, chunkily ripe red in an age when too many Aussie Shirazes are looking a bit dilute and washed out.

71   2008 Pinot Noir, Gunboat Point, Central Otago, New Zealand, 14.5% abv

Laithwaites, £14.99

Central Otago is New Zealand's most southerly vineyard region, high up in the Southern Alps snowfields. The Pinot styles here are more extreme than anywhere else in New Zealand, some verging on the aggressive, but there are pockets of surprising gentleness too, and this is one of them. In fact, it's scented in a rather charming old-fashioned way; its damson and cherry fruit has a contemplative sweetness and the tannin and acid are as if you were thoughtfully chewing the skins of an autumn ripe plum.

72   2009 Sauvignon Blanc, Tinpot Hut, Marlborough, New Zealand, 13% abv

Liberty Wines, Villeneuve Wines, Noel Young Wines, £9.99

Too many New Zealand Sauvignons are starting to taste bland and inoffensive. Tinpot Hut isn't one of them. It's tangy, aggressive, invigorating – just what I want from a Kiwi Sauvignon. One reason is that the grapes mostly grow in the Blind River area, where conditions are hard and bony. But above all, the producers don't compromise. We want a wine full of green leaf, green apple peel, nettle, coffee bean and lime zest attack – but with a ripe texture flowing through
it – and that's exactly what
Tinpot Hut gives us.

73 2008 Pinot Noir, Whirlpool Reach, Tamar River, Tasmania, Australia, 14% abv

 Oddbins, £10.99

Australia struggles to find conditions that really suit Pinot Noir. Tasmania provides the answer. Down in the river valleys, protected from the worst of the weather, Tasmanians can enjoy long, warm, balmy summers and autumns that never get really hot. Pinot loves that and it shows in this wine, which has a beautiful gentle feel and a soft, beguiling flavour of strawberry, peach and pink apple flesh scented by late summer honeysuckle.

74 2007 Ribera del Duero, El Lagar de Isilla, Castilla y León, Spain, 14.5% abv

 Stone, Vine & Sun, £9.95

It's often the cheaper Ribera del Dueros which have the purest fruit and the greatest expression of these fabulous Spanish vineyards because they're not swamped with vanilla oak, and they've been made to drink at table, not to impress millionaire collectors. This is rich, strong and packed with blackcurrant and black plum fruit and lightly touched by spicy oak that allows the scent of the fruit to come through. It's a delight now, but will be more of a beauty in five years or so.

75 2009 'Springvale', Watervale Riesling, Grosset, Clare Valley, South Australia, 12.5% abv

 Liberty Wines, Wine Society, Noel Young Wines, £17.99

Jeffrey Grosset is arguably Australia's greatest Riesling producer. In less good years like 2008 his wines sing with excitement as soon as they leave the vat. In great years like 2009, when the wine will have a 20-year lifespan ahead, they tend to be more closed in and reserved for a year or two. This is strong and citrus, with a whisper of mint and anise and a prickle of spritz. Good and lean now, it will be a thrilling, scented classic in a few years' time.

76 2009 Dornfelder Trocken, Kollmann-Lex, Mosel, Germany, 12.5% abv

♟ Nick Dobson Wines, £10.95

Red wines in the Mosel, whatever next? Red grapes need warmth and sun to ripen and the ultra-cool Mosel has always been a light white domain. Yet here we are in the very good Riesling village of Klüsserath with a really lovely red. If that isn't proof of global warming... Actually Dornfelder performs best when it's not too hot and this is a lovely ripe yet cool style, scented with apple blossom and orchard leaves, flowing with a plum and apple juice sweetness and acidity that softens its minerality and fades away to a scented lingering aftertaste.

77 2009 Grüner Veltliner, Messwein-Celebritas, Salomon Undhof, Kremstal, Austria, 13% abv

♀ Lea & Sandeman, £11.95

As pale and bright as a wine can be. Pale apple core, pale lemon leaf scent, mineral dust on pale spring sunshine, white-fleshed fruit, a cool breeze drifting through the wine and scattering the merest drop or two of grapefruit oil onto its surface. There's a little spritz, too – it's like drinking springtime.

78 2008 Malbec, Amalaya, Bodegas Colomé, Valle Calchaquí, Salta, Argentina, 14.5% abv

♟ Majestic, £8.99

The higher you go up the Andes, the fresher, the more focused the fruit in your wine, and the more penetrating the scent. You can't go much higher than the Calchaquí Valley right up near the Bolivian border, and you'll be hard put to find a livelier, more perfumed Malbec than this. It has a heady aroma of violets and rose petals as well as sweet damson fruit; this carries on in its flavour – deep piercing damson fruit delightfully scented with flowers and softened by just enough oak, a touch of appetizing pepper bitterness and a flash of the trademark Malbec perfume of fresh new leather.

79 2007 Carmenère-Cabernet Sauvignon, Novas, Emiliana, Colchagua Valley, Chile, 14.5% abv
♟ Booths, Vintage Roots, £7.75

Emiliana are the original organic pioneers in Chile and they continue to produce remarkable quality for a very affordable price. The people in the vineyards and winery are full of passion and belief. Just try this excellent dark, superripe red. Superripe yes, but not overripe, always in excellent balance between luscious blackberry and blackcurrant fruit, a trail of jasmine scent sprinkled with spice, and the restraining hand of coal dust tannin.

80 2007 Saint-Joseph, Nicolas Perrin, Rhône Valley, France, 13% abv
♟ Wine Society, £17

The heart of St-Joseph, opposite Hermitage in the towering reaches of the northern Rhône Valley, is an awesome vineyard site. Though politicians have vastly expanded the St-Joseph appellation onto flatter, inferior sites, the best, most scented wines come from the original cliffs and slopes. This example delivers a haunting perfume of violet, lily stems and drifting coal smoke which combines with aromatic blueberry and blackberry fruit and a fine coating of creamy oak to make a really smashing, classy mouthful of Rhône red.

81   2006 Vacqueyras, Carmin Brillant, Le Clos de Caveau, Rhône Valley, France, 14.6% abv

♥ Vintage Roots, £15.50

Vacqueyras is an excellent village just down the road from Châteauneuf-du-Pape, making pretty similar wines at a much lower price. If you want powerful, beefy wine just the right side of OTT, Vacqueyras is a pretty good place to look for it. This wine is brooding and dark, full of chocolate, date and prune black sweetness, yet it also boasts a streak of metallic freshness and a fair bit of a scent like the warm brush on southern French hillsides.

82   2008 Furmint, Patricius, Tokaji, Hungary, 13% abv

♀ Great Western Wine, £9.95

Furmint is the grape that is the main player in the sweet wine, Tokaji; in its drier manifestations it has a reputation for scything acidity and tartness. Yet this dry Furmint turns out to be something of a pussycat. It does have acidity, but it isn't fierce. Indeed the wine seems to be a paean to the mellow fruitfulness of autumn – a lovely combination of goldengage jam and autumn fruits fallen from the bough, oozing their nectar and praying to be gathered before the wasps descend, and this is spread upon brioche, then coated with honeycomb.

83   2008 Bourgogne Chardonnay, Domaine Jomain, Burgundy, France, 13% abv

♀ Majestic, £10.99

The name and address on the label says it all. Domaine Jomain, Puligny-Montrachet. Finding a grower in a top village with a few excess barrels that don't quite fit into his other blends is the key to drinking fine white Burgundy at a fair price. This doesn't have the majesty and depth of a top-line Puligny, but in its lighter, understated way it is classic Burgundy: oatmeal and banana softness, sharpened by good lemon acid and given an almost salty savoury flavour of hazelnut that is true Puligny-Montrachet.

84   2008 Viognier, Zaca Mesa, Santa Ynez Valley, California, USA, 14.5% abv
♀ Great Western Wine, £17.50

Viognier was once seen as the great white hope of Californian whites as Chardonnay struggled to cope with the heat of the Golden West. But Viognier found the sunny conditions equally difficult to tame, and too many examples are oily and fat. However, there are some areas, such as Santa Ynez in Santa Barbara County, where marginally cooler conditions allow the tropical fruit flavours to flourish alongside some heady perfume. This is certainly fat and plush, but its rich oozing apricot fruit is given welcome support by pear orchard blossom and fresh leather scent, as well as a hint of the bitterness you'd get from chewing apricot skin.

85   2008 Carignan, T.H, Cauquenes-Loncomilla, Undurraga, Maule, Chile, 14% abv
♀ Wine Society, £10.95

The revival of Carignan worldwide as a serious grape has been a delight. Chile has done its bit by re-discovering, and then cherishing and fostering, ancient Carignan vines in the southern part of the country, and several companies are now making excellent wines from them. Ripe cranberry and redcurrant mark this wine out, as ripe as you can get such acid red fruits, and a shiny stones texture that almost polishes your tooth enamel. I'd like a bit less oak, but that will integrate over the next six months.

86   2008 Syrah, Sacred Hill, Hawkes Bay, New Zealand, 12.5% abv

🍷 Sainsbury's, £8.99

An excellent example of the way Syrah from the deep stony vineyards of Gimblett Gravels in Hawkes Bay can develop a soft, ripe texture yet retain the chilly flavours of this cool region. The wine is almost velvety soft and manages to mix both red and white wine flavours quite beautifully. White pepper, green celery, pale golden plums and lily stems are totally at ease with the soft yet cool heart of chocolate flakes, chocolate wafers, cocoa, red plums and cream.

87   2008 Shiraz or Syrah, M. Chapoutier, Domaine Tournon, Western Victoria, Australia, 14.5% abv

🍷 Oddbins, £14.49

It's great to see an important company like Chapoutier taking the cooler parts of Australia seriously. Chapoutier is one of the star producers of the northern Rhône, and it has now turned its hand to the ancient red soils of Heathcote. The result is this lovely blackberry-fruited charmer; its lush body is slightly roughened up with grainy tannin; there's a slight savoury scent of woodsmoke and crème fraîche, but the finish is all black fruit.

88   2008 Chablis Premier Cru, Côte de Lechet, Vincent Dampt, Burgundy, France, 13% abv

♀ Corney & Barrow, £18.99

Real, high-quality Chablis is a balm to the soul. The Premier Crus are mostly a little riper than they were a decade ago, but they still appear unadorned, unbejewelled, in a white wine world where alcohol and oak are too much in the ascendant. The ripeness here shows in some creamy texture and a hint of honey, but even such flavours seem to have a stony rub to them; the lemon acidity seems to be squeezed through stones. Chablis prides itself on minerality. This wine demonstrates what the word means.

89   2007 Old Vine Zinfandel, Lodi, Ravenswood, California, USA, 14.5% abv
♟ Majestic, Sainsbury's, Spar, Wine Society and others, around £9

Lodi is a warm, well-watered area in California's Sacramento River delta, which specializes in ripe, soft, balanced red wines. The Zinfandel is especially good, and this is a lush yet rather old-timer brew of stewed black fruit and bramble jelly churned about with dates, raisins, a leather belt or two and the wood shavings from a carpenter's lathe.

90   2007 Ventoux, Domaine des Anges, Rhône Valley, France, 14.5% abv
♟ Big Red Wine Company, £7.65

British-owned Domaine des Anges has been showing the locals how to make fresh, scented quaffable reds at a fair price for decades. 2007 was a particularly good vintage, and this is ripe and full, but seductively scented with cool orchard air, and the dark red fruit of cherries and strawberries flows effortlessly through the local landscape of rocks and herbs.

91 2007 Côtes du Rhône (Syrah-Grenache), Mas Arnaud, Rhône Valley, France, 13.5% abv

The Colchester Wine Company, £8.29

I've never had a red cherry and loganberry crumble. Has anyone? Well, that's what this wine made me think of – lush, juicy raspberries and loganberries and scented red cherries, all stirred together with some kitchen spice, then topped with crumble as only your mum knows how. So next time you go home for Sunday lunch, ask her to make the crumble, and bring her a bottle of this as a pressie.

92 2009 Gamay Noir, Woodthorpe Vineyard, Te Mata Estate, Hawkes Bay, New Zealand, 13% abv

Oxford Wine Company, Wine Society, £12.99

Te Mata is a very posh New Zealand winery, famous for serious long-lasting reds and whites. So where does Gamay, the grape of Beaujolais, of flirting and fun, fit in? Maybe after spending all day slaving away at really challenging stuff, they needed a bright and breezy quaffer to relax with. So they made this Gamay: lovely peach, cherry and strawberry fruit, and a creamy texture roughened up by stones and a ripe apple acidity.

93 2006 Riesling Spätlese, Kreuznacher Krötenpfuhl, Dönnhoff, Nahe, Germany, 8% abv

Waitrose, £18.99

Dönnhoff is one of Germany's greatest winemakers, so if anyone can draw out the essence of the frog pond, he can. Krötenpfuhl – frog pond – is the name of the vineyard; they have some very strange vineyard names in Germany. Never

fear, the wine's a delight – quite mature, and probably made in a style that hasn't changed for 50 years – quite sweet, packed with flavour, very low in alcohol. Beautifully honeyed, peachy, with an aroma of leather, the rustle of pebbles on a stream-bed and an almost sweaty richness like the crust on a pot of clotted cream.

94 2007 Saint-Aubin Blanc, Françoise & Denis Clair, Burgundy, France, 13% abv
♀ Stone, Vine & Sun, £15.75

Saint-Aubin, just outside Burgundy's main stretch of villages, produces wines very similar to those of top villages like Chassagne-Montrachet, but just a little more reserved. It has some mild oatmeal scent, a mild butter shortbread finish, and some lemon acidity to keep it fresh. It's good now, but I'd be tempted to keep a bottle or two for two to five years. Côte d'Or Burgundy flavour for just under £16.

95 2005 Pécharmant, Château de Tiregand, South-West France, 14% abv
♥ Tanners, £10.95

Pécharmant is a very obscure little nook in Bergerac, but it had a positively Bordeaux-like reputation a few generations ago – looking at the charmingly archaic label, I don't think they've employed a designer since World War II. Using the Bordeaux grape varieties (Merlot, Cabernet Sauvignon, Cabernet Franc, Malbec) this is dense, rich, serious red, full of sweet black fruit overlaid with a cream cheesy savouriness and a thwack of tannin. You should really treat this like a top 2005 Bordeaux – I'd lay it down for 10–15 years, but, wow, will it be good when you finally stumble over it under the stairs.

96 2005 Collio Goriziano, Clivi Brazan, I Clivi di Ferdinando Zanusso, Friuli, Italy, 13.5% abv
♀ Lea & Sandeman, £14.75

Tocai is widely planted around north-east Italy and either makes dull bland wines or intriguing wines depending on the ambition and talents of the producer. These guys coax every last bit of personality out of the grape and have created a fascinating, soft yet slightly bitter white. The softness is of baked apples and fresh-from-the-oven buns, maybe some creamy yeast too, while the bitterness is of persimmon skins and grated apple skins, tempered by wax and soft leather.

97 2009 Chiroubles, Domaine de la Chapelle des Bois (C & E Coudert-Appert), Beaujolais, France, 13% abv
♀ Stone, Vine & Sun, £10.50

Gorgeous, juicy red, so typical of the excellent 2009 vintage: strawberries and peaches, cherries and chocolate in a riotous merry-go-round of flailing peppercorns and stems, drowning in the torrent of lush red fruit.

98 2007 Corbières, Château de Sérame, Languedoc, France, 13% abv
🍷 Handford Wines, £7.99

It's nice to find a Corbières with a little maturity, because these mountain reds age brilliantly if you give them a chance. This has sweet, dark fruit – blackberry and plums – ripped by rough herbs, soothed by blossomy scent and darkened with licorice.

99 2009 Carchelo, Bodegas Carchelo, Jumilla, Murcia, Spain, 14% abv
🍷 Great Northern Wine, £9.99; Oddbins, £10.99

They could never have made a wine as fresh as this is in Jumilla a decade ago, but that shows the amazing rate of change in Spain's less well-known areas. This is actually scented – not easy in the baking south – and although there is a touch of quite pleasant raisin fruit there, it's outgunned by richer fresh plum and a little floral scent that seasons its soft, lush, syrupy texture.

100 2007 Saint-Chinian (Syrah-Grenache), 'Les Fleurs Sauvages', Château de Combebelle, Languedoc, France, 14% abv
🍷 Oddbins, £10.99

I like this wine's name: 'the wild flowers' – wild mountain flowers, I'd say, from the unkempt mountain slopes around St-Chinian. These floral scents are joined by the pungent aromas of wild herbs and anise from the garrigue, and they're all packed into this powerful heady red, rich with plum fruit, scratched by grainy tannin.

50 FOR AROUND A TENNER

There's no doubt that some sections of our wine market are suffering in these tough times. Good wines at under £4 are few (I've recommended a tight little bunch on pages 96–102) and the hallowed £4.99 price point has been squeezed and squeezed (we've moved our limit for everyday wines to £6 this year – see pages 82–95). But the area of 'around a tenner' – by which I mean more than £6.50 but not much more than a tenner – has become a cauldron of opportunity and excitement. Less fashionable grape varieties and areas offer wonderful drinking here if you're prepared to be adventurous. Producers in more fashionable areas are finding people won't pay inflated prices any more. But if they don't prune so severely – so that each vine has more bunches of grapes – use less expensive oak, or maybe even sell wine under a different label to 'preserve the integrity' of their brand…well, the good wines are still out there at prices we can afford. Don't let the economic crisis kill your spirit. Now's the time to fight back by drinking savvy: drinking better for less.

• In this section you will find white wines first, then reds, in descending price order.

WHITE WINE

2009 Vernaccia di San Gimignano, Le Calcinaie, Tuscany, Italy, 12.5% abv Goedhuis, £10.28

This is in effect the local white wine of the Chianti region. It's quite full, with a kind of oatmeal cheese biscuit savouriness, but that's challenged by tasty yet lean chewy apple peel and dried apple slices mixed with aniseed and grapefruit, and a spritzy prickle on your tongue.

2009 Sauvignon Blanc, Greenhough, Nelson, New Zealand, 13% abv Colchester Wine Company, £10.25

Marlborough is the best-known region for New Zealand Sauvignon, but just an hour or so's drive away is the charming, almost idyllic, small wine region of Nelson where they make excellent Sauvignon that is perhaps a little leaner and more refreshing than a lot of current offerings from Marlborough. This has a tiny prickle of spritz to prepare your palate for a delightfully gentle yet tart flavour of green apple flesh, blackcurrant leaf, orchard blossom and the pith and zest of a ripe Sicilian lemon.

2007 Château Le Chec, Graves, Bordeaux, France, 12.5% abv Adnams, £9.99

Delightful, fresh, full-flavoured white Bordeaux. Fermentation in oak barrels has added an attractive custardy weight and brioche crust softness to the white peach and nectarine fruit. I've said it before, I'll say it again – Bordeaux makes wonderful, affordable dry whites.

2009 Chenin Blanc, The Den, Painted Wolf, Coastal Region, South Africa, 14.5% abv Cambridge Wine Merchants, Flagship Wines, Great Western Wine, £9.99

Chenin from South Africa is making quite a name for itself. Admittedly a lot of cheap Cape whites are Chenin-based – that's because Chenin is South Africa's most widely planted variety – but when the vines are old, the crops small and the winemaking skilful, lovely wines result. This is round, mellow, delightfully easy to enjoy, with a honeysuckle and kitchen spice scent, mild apple fruit and just a nip of apple pip bitterness.

2009 Falanghina, Terredora, Campania, Italy, 13% abv
Majestic, £9.99

A really good example of why everyone's starting to talk about the Falanghina grape. This is pretty wild: 'funky old baba cake dough, medlars, fresh country dust and baked apple skins gone brown and crinkly' were some of my notes. There's some peach and pear syrup and good acidity, and when you realize these wild flavours are just suggestions, almost pale in reality, you've got a fascinating white in your glass.

2009 Sauvignon Blanc, De Grendel, Coastal Region, South Africa, 13.5% abv Oddbins, £9.99

South African Sauvignons are marvellously different from the New Zealand ones we've become accustomed to. They are less tamed, more rough-edged, less predictable, with the wild rocks and surging waves of the Cape's west coast seeming to form their personalities. This is marvellously raw in its leafiness, its mineral rock scent, and its spritzy tickle of carbon dioxide, but the fruit is ripe – an attractive slightly squashy green apple fleshiness rounded off with some breadcrust softness.

2009 Sauvignon Blanc, Leyda, Garuma Vineyard, Leyda Valley, Chile, 14% abv
Oddbins, £9.99

In the Garuma vineyard you stand with your face to the blazing sun yet your body is whipped by the sea frets and the ocean gales that race inland from the nearby Pacific. It's a magic combination – the sun fully ripening the grapes, yet the chill winds packing the wine with the vibrant green flavours of lime zest and capsicum and gooseberry, and showering the fruit with the clean dry scents of stones and summer earth.

2008 Vin de Savoie, Chignin, Domaine Gilles Berlioz, Savoie, France, 11.5% abv
Wine Society, £9.95

Merchants say Savoie wines are difficult to sell in Britain, even though lots of us drink them when we're skiing in the Alps. That's such a pity, because they really chime with the times – they're lean, they're tangy, and they're low in alcohol. Which all adds up to a gentle but bone dry white, with a flavour of green apple flesh and the shy acidity of boiled lemons, scented with mountain herbs and the merest suggestion of tobacco.

2008 Unwooded Chardonnay, Mad Bay, Howard Park Wines, Western Australia, 13.5% abv
Tesco, £9.29

Made by the top-rated Howard Park winery in Western Australia, this is an appetizing example of how attractive Chardonnay can be when it is not aged in oak barrels. You get the naked Chardonnay, without the vanilla and spice; this is lightly perfumed, a slight pot-pourri kind of scent, full of melon and ripe apple fruit, with a dry stony rub and a lick of honey.

2008 Chenin Blanc, Secateurs, Badenhorst Family Wines, Swartland, South Africa, 14% abv Oxford Wine Company, £8.99

The quality of South African Chenin depends to a large extent on where the grapes grow – these Chenin grapes grow on old bush vines on granite mountains in Swartland, north of Cape Town. That's where South Africa's best old vines are, both red and white. Enjoy this for its gentle baked apple fruit, grated lemon peel bitter acid bite, and crème fraîche and rum baba syrupy party softness.

2008 Riesling, Verus, Stajerska, Slovenia, 13% abv
Real Wine Co, £8.99

Slovenia is quietly creeping into our wine consciousness and could become a significant player for elegant, cool-climate whites in a few years' time. This Riesling shows why. The label says it is dry – I'd say 'not quite' – the style is bright, with a spritzy prickle, a scent of leather and peppercorn, anise and green leaves and a gentle mildly honeyed flavour nicely balanced by fresh acidity.

2009 Sauvignon Blanc, La Grande Cuvée, Dourthe, Bordeaux, France, 12.5% abv Majestic, £8.99

My fellow wine writers must have more time on their hands than me: Jamie Goode and Tim Atkin have been out to Bordeaux to help blend this white – and the result is impressive. Bordeaux whites are one of France's unsung treasures; this one is bright, juicy and dry, the texture is ripe but not at all heavy, and the flavour is streaks of green leaf, lemon zest and ripe grapefruit scratched by the mineral sharpness of flint.

2008 Sauvignon Saint-Bris, Clotilde Davenne, Burgundy, France, 12.5% abv
From Vineyards Direct, £8.95

This is a fascinating wine – Sauvignon Blanc grown in the virtually Chardonnay-only confines of northern Burgundy, next to Chablis. This is as lean and chalky as a Chablis, yet pinging with lemony acidity and the chewiness of green apple peel, as well as showing a surprising squashy greengage fruit that no Chablis would be caught sporting.

2009 Torrontés, Mauricio Lorca, Famatina Vineyards, La Rioja, Argentina, 14% abv
Private Cellar, £8.75

Torrontés is Argentina's signature white grape. At one time it prided itself on making wines vaguely reminiscent of celestial loo-cleaner, but the last year or two have seen increasing numbers of producers fathom how to make the best of it. Here's a good example: a wine with a rich, fat feel, wafts of heady perfume, and ripe pear juice and peach flesh fruit cut through with the perfumed acidity of grapefruit marmalade and lime zest.

2009 Sauvignon Blanc, Vin de Pays Charentais, Domaine Gardrat, France, 11.5% abv
Yapp Brothers, £8.50

With France making Sauvignon like this, I could be waving goodbye to the Kiwis – for a week or two at any rate. This comes from Cognac country: chilly acres, but in 2009 just perfect for making snappy whites. It doesn't seem totally ripe – the best Sauvignons don't – yet the texture is full, the flavour is juicy green apple, stewed gooseberry and crunchy green capsicum, and the acidity is lemony and lean.

2009 Riesling, Tingleup Vineyard (Howard Park Wines), Great Southern, Western Australia, 12% abv
Tesco Finest, £8.49

Western Australia really is making its mark over here. For a long time we hardly saw its wines and the excuse was 'there isn't enough to export'. New vineyards now mean good supplies of beautifully flavoured, fairly priced reds and, especially, whites. This is gentler than some Aussie Rieslings, but the flavours are tangy – lemon and lime zest, orange juice acidity and underripe white peach with slightly sweet stewed apple flesh.

2009 Rueda Verdejo, Carrasviñas, Bodegas Félix Lorenzo Cachazo, Castilla y León, Spain, 12.5% abv
Great Western Wine, Swig, £8.35

Despite being just up the road from the red wine powerhouse of Toro, where the red grapes virtually bake on the vine, Rueda has based its reputation on its ability to produce snappy, fresh whites at low alcohol levels. This wine is dusty, windblown, mineral; you can feel the aridity of the place, but it's reflected in gaunt but appetizing green apple, lemon zest and ripe grapefruit tanginess, with just a drop or two of sweat from the brow of a thirsty vineyard worker.

2009 Falanghina, Giardini, Puglia, Italy, 12.5% abv
Sainsbury's, £7.99

Falanghina is a southern Italian white grape that has 'future star' written all over it, because of its lovely delicate floral scent and apricot and grapefruit flavour. This example is a little more funky than some – less floral but still scented – and its rich fruit is kept in check by the undertow of stony minerality.

2007 Sauvignon Blanc-Semillon, Houghton, Western Australia, 12.5% abv Tesco, £7.49

Very classy white at this price. The blend of grape varieties that makes the great Bordeaux whites seems to be fabulously suited to Western Australia. This is really tangy, almost ozone-scented stuff: sea-washed, sun-bleached pebbles; citrus zest; white apple flesh with a dash of coffee; and a texture halfway to green capsicum syrup.

2008 Saint Mont, South-West France, 12.5% abv Marks & Spencer, £6.99

The south-west of France is an excellent stomping ground if you're looking for crisp, tangy whites. This wine uses local grape varieties: Gros Manseng, Petit Courbu and Arrufiac. It doesn't have quite the leafy zip of Sauvignon – the varieties aren't so aromatic – but you get a very bright mouthful of apple flesh and green leaf acidity, smoothed by some nut savouriness and by pebbles that seem to have been washed in cream.

2009 Sauvignon Blanc, Darling (Ormonde Cellars), South Africa, 13% abv Tesco Finest, £6.99

This is relatively soft in texture for a Sauvignon, but makes up for that with a zesty, tangy flavour of blackcurrant leaf, nettle and bone-dry earth and a bright, summery fruit flavour like fluffy eating apple flesh.

2009 Sauvignon Blanc, Six Hats, Fairtrade, Western Cape, South Africa, 14% abv Booths, £6.99

Six Hats is a very good addition to the Fairtrade ranks. This movement is making an enormous difference in South Africa, taking community after community out of poverty, and with wines this good we have no excuse not to support it. This wine really captures the Cape Sauvignon style – quite aggressive in its tangy bite, with a chewy green pepper, nettle and coffee bean flavour, and a lean, lemon zesty acidity.

RED WINE

2006 Cabernet Sauvignon-Merlot, Mill Race, Vergelegen, Stellenbosch, South Africa, 14.5% abv
Cambridge Wine Merchants, Colchester Wine Co, Flagship Wines, Majestic, Morrisons, Swig, c.£10

Vergelegen is a really swish South African operation, so this Cabernet-Merlot blend is excellent value at around a tenner. It's nicely mature, and packed with plum and blackcurrant fruit, scented with anise and mint, blackened with licorice and rounded out with coconut.

2007 Côtes du Rhône-Villages, Le Ponnant, La Ferme du Mont, Rhône Valley, France, 14.5% abv Real Wine Co, £9.99

Buy the 2007 Rhônes while you can. We've seen a lot of good vintages in the Rhône Valley during the past few years, but 2007 combined monumental ripeness with a startling acid freshness. This example – full of cherry and plum fruit, a splash of dates, a daub of cream, a swish of herbs, bright and scented – shows how.

2009 Pinot Noir, Punto Niño, Laroche, Casablanca Valley, Chile, 14.5% abv
Liberty Wines, £9.99

Laroche are basically Chablis experts in France, but Michel Laroche has always been a restless innovator roaming far outside the tiny boundaries of Chablis, so I'm not surprised to see him turning up in what is Chile's original cool-climate site, between Santiago and the Pacific. He's made a Pinot Noir with a hint of lushness, quite rich strawberry fruit and the mellowness of cream, but underscored by mouthwatering stony dryness.

2009 Valpolicella, Allegrini, Veneto, Italy, 13% abv
Bennetts Fine Wines, Liberty Wines, Stainton Wines, Wine Society, £9.99

One of the great names in Italian reds, Allegrini makes a variety of wild and wonderful special Valpolicella cuvées, but this is their bread and butter wine. Well, that makes it sound a bit mundane, yet this is anything but – a beautifully scented, mild-natured red, full of fresh-picked cherries and plums, brushed by leather and made even more appetizing by the cool kiss of riverbed pebbles.

2008 Cabernet Sauvignon, Steak House, The Magnificent Wine Company, Columbia Valley, Washington, USA, 13% abv
Co-op, £9.49

We don't see many Washington State wines over here, but they've got a big reputation Stateside for power and focused fruit. This is pretty gutsy and the tannins are a bit aggressive – it *is* called Steak House and that's where it would be most at home – but there's a nice spicy feel to the wine and the fruit is bright and fat and plummy.

2008 Cabernet Sauvignon, Wakefield, Clare Valley, South Australia, 14% abv
Majestic, £9.49

Wakefield is a winery on the up. It has been around for a long time and it owns a vast tract of vines in the Clare Valley, but it has never been consistent. Well, their current red releases are very good. This is really tasty, traditional Clare

Cabernet – full of blackcurrant fruit and black cherry skins, mint and minerals and a nice waxy, almost syrupy, consistency.

• The Shiraz is the same price and is a rich chocolate, toffee and coconut mouthful.

2008 Pinot Noir, Marlborough, New Zealand, 13.5% abv
Asda Extra Special, £9.20

This is an Asda own-label from the trendy Wither Hills winery. And it shows. It's classy Pinot: gentle, mellow, strawberry fruit mixed with banana – I remember banana and strawberry jam sandwiches from when I was a kid – some breadcrust and cream softness undercut with a stony dryness. With a Wither Hills label you'd be paying quite a few quid more.

2008 Côtes du Rhône, Belleruche (Grenache-Syrah), M. Chapoutier, Rhône Valley, France, 13.5% abv
Majestic, £8.99

Belleruche has become one of France's most reliable high-volume Côtes du Rhone reds. And not just reliable – it has real class too. Scented with herbs, anise and peppertree blossom, roughened just a little with warm stones and full of the ripe red flavours of strawberry and crimson plums, this is the real thing.

2008 Côtes du Roussillon, Domaine de l'Oranger, Roussillon, France, 14% abv
Averys, £8.99

Côtes du Roussillon reds can sometimes taste just too ripe and baked for their own good, but not this one. You do get an attractive date-y warmth and a soft lush texture that had me thinking of a good paté(!), but to go with that there's a delightfully unexpected orange scent and orange peel flavour (it's not auto-suggestion from its name; perhaps the vineyard is on the site of the old orange grove), good black fruit, a swish of herbs and a brusque, rocky dryness.

2007 Rioja, Single Vineyard, Ramón Bilbao, Spain, 13.5% abv
Majestic, £8.99

A rarity – single-vineyard Rioja: most Riojas are blends of different vineyards and villages made up in winery cellars. I'd say this is a charming old-fashioned vineyard, giving ripe soft strawberry fruit that marries effortlessly with gentle vanilla toffee oak and just the hint of a rough edge to create a glass of really nice old-style Rioja.

2007 Cacc'e Mmitte di Lucera, Pezzagrande, Masseria Celentano, Puglia, Italy, 13% abv
Lea & Sandeman, £8.95

The best thing to do here is not to try to understand the label, not to try to work out where it comes from – somewhere in Italy – not to try to work out the grape varieties – various obscure Italian ones – just open the bottle and wallow in a strange but delicious concoction that could almost masquerade as an oddball Burgundy with its waxy texture and strawberry fruit, yet you'll have to factor in the dusty butterscotch, leathery barley sugar and rocks as well. I'd just drink it and devil take the details.

2007 Bordeaux, Château la Fleur Coterie, France, 13% abv
Goedhuis, £8.71

This little property is based in the very good but unsung and undervalued Fronsac region to the east of Bordeaux, next to the very good, very famous, and overpriced Pomerol area. That's what gives it some real class – quite rich, scented plum fruit, an attractive appetizing earthiness, some tannic roughness and fairly creamy oak. Good now, it'll be even better in five years.

2006 Cabernet Sauvignon, Tsantali, Halkidiki, Greece, 14.5% abv
Waitrose, £8.49

A chance to help the Greeks cut their deficit as well as experience a genuinely different style of Cabernet. Greek wines really do taste different to those of western Europe – they're more austere, starker in outline, sterner in character. This reminds me of stones baked in the Adriatic heat, ripe fruit blackened on the vine, plums and cherries stewed and mashed together with prunes but wrapped in a sultry, yeasty, weighty soft cocoon.

2006 Claret La Reserve, Bordeaux, France, 12.5% abv
From Vineyards Direct, £8.45

Very nice, affordable red made by Jonathan Maltus, one of the super-premium second-mortgage-required 'garagiste' producers of St-Émilion who create 'mini-crus' of negligible amounts of concentrated reds they then sell for astronomical prices. This is what he'd drink for a midweek lunch – rather old-fashioned, fat, glyceriny-textured fruit, a bit savoury, yet creamy; only the tannic chewiness is a bit on the modern side.

2006 Crozes-Hermitage, Cave de Tain, Rhône Valley, France, 12.5% abv
Tesco Finest, £7.99

This is made by the co-op at Tain l'Hermitage, a big operation that controls the majority of the vines in Crozes-Hermitage in the northern Rhône. Until quite recently it had a kind of 'British supermarkets vat' that basically contained the stewy cheap stuff that no one else wanted. But there's been a sea change at the co-op and the quality has improved out of all recognition. This is full of solid black plum and blackberry fruit, a certain creaminess of texture, and a lively graphite and peppercorn bone-dry aroma. Good Crozes.

2009 Grande Réserve de Gassac, Vin de Pays de l'Hérault, Languedoc-Roussillon, France, 13.5% abv
Laithwaites, £7.99

This comes from the very serious and expensive stable of Mas de Daumas Gassac, the most famous and pricey red wine in the French Midi. It's sort of a baby brother, but despite being very young, this is a sophisticated mouthful. At the moment it's almost purple-fruited and sprinkled with warm mineral dust, but this will soon develop into a rich black fruit syrup of cherry and plums, ripe and scented and wonderfully easy to drink.

2007 Grenache, Willunga 100, McLaren Vale, South Australia, 14.5% abv
Sainsbury's, £7.99

Grenache red has gotta give you fun. By the bucketload. And this does. Riproaring stuff, unapologetic, unabashed happy juice dripping with strawberry and loganberry syrup, sharpened up with cranberry juice acidity and whacked with hillside herbs.

2008 Malbec, Pascual Toso, Mendoza, Argentina, 14% abv
Noel Young Wines, £7.99

This shows the glorious paradox of Argentine Malbec. The fruit seems sultry, heavy-limbed, almost baked on the vine, yet the wine is succulently scented with violet and ripe sweet damson syrup. It's a magic, hedonistic combination and I'm delighted to see Argentina getting the hang of it at an affordable price level.

2008 Malbec Reserve, Alma Andina, Mendoza, Argentina, 14% abv
Laithwaites, £7.99

Gorgeous, chubby-cheeked red from the Malbec grape. Malbec likes Argentina's warm conditions, but can bake if the heat gets too much. This comes from high vineyards towards the Andes and so you get as much dark plummy fruit, as much chocolate cream and cocoa dust, as much sweet oak spice as you could want, but the wine never tastes baked, and always retains its freshness.

2008 Pinotage, Beyers Truter, Stellenbosch, South Africa, 14.5% abv
Tesco Finest, £7.99

They call Beyers Truter the Pinotage king in South Africa, and it's a title he's worked hard to earn. Pinotage does have fabulous flavours hiding inside its dark skin, but it isn't easy to unlock the grape's magic. Well, this is what it should taste like: ripe, almost stewy, mulberry and black plum fruit, definitely tinged with bonfire smoke, fattened up with some toasted marshmallow and with a rich yet serious texture like sugarless syrup.

2008 Syrah-Aragonês-Alicante, Valoroso, Casa Ermelinda Freitas, Península de Setúbal, Portugal, 14.5% abv
Laithwaites, £7.99

Setúbal, just south of Lisbon, is famous for sweet Muscat wines, but its future lies in ripe, tasty reds. This is a three-grape blend, led by Syrah, and it's a big, full, spicy wine. Its fruit is rough chopped and its oak sweetness is a bit rough hewn, but it's a good, dense red with the intriguing flavour of cherry cake lingering on the tongue.

2008 Stickleback Red, Heartland, South Australia, 14.5% abv
Cambridge Wine Merchants, Great Western Wine, Stone, Vine & Sun, Villeneuve Wines, Wine Society, £7.95

A very encouraging, innovative blend from Australia: Australia's top red performers Shiraz and Cabernet, mixed with Dolcetto from Italy's north-west and Lagrein from way up in the Dolomite mountain passes. I'm delighted to see experimentation with Italian varieties becoming more

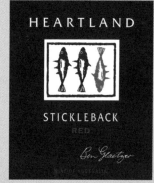

widespread in Australia, and this is a really interesting red, smelling of eucalyptus and lime and tree bark and boasting a loose-limbed flavour of baked blackcurrants and plums, savoury grilled meat and lively lime zest acidity.

2008 Douro (Quinta do Crasto), Portugal, 13.5% abv
Sainsbury's Taste the Difference, £7.52

This is always one of the classier bargains at Sainsbury's. The trendy and exciting Quinta do Crasto allows Sainsbury's to take a selection of barrels for their own label. The resulting wine is usually less dense, less oaky, less alcoholic than the estate's main label; a bit more of a glugger, but still serious. It's quite deep enough, quite powerful in a kind of rock syrup way, but it has very attractive fruit – purple-black plums and black cherry skins – and a scent that mingles violets with hillside herbs, and whatever minimal oak it has is kept well in the background.

2008 Carmenere, Karu Estate, Colchagua Valley, Chile, 13.5% abv
Virgin Wines, £6.99

Carmenère has a savage side and a cultured side: either way, the flavours are big and impressive. This is a good-tempered Carmenère, massaged into a scented, spicy style, yet still serious. It's full of excellent dark plum and blackberry fruit, a touch of scent hovers over the glass, and there's a quiet savoury growl from something like peppercorn – but not at all savage.

2009 Malbec, Viñalta, Argentina, 14% abv
Marks & Spencer, £6.99

Made for M&S by the high-quality Fabre Montmayou/Domaine Vistalba operation from grapes grown high up towards the Andes at 1200 metres. This is unoaked, so you get all the fruit head on, and it's textbook Malbec – deep and ripe, with just enough tannic bitterness to match the big plum fruit, the plum skins chewiness and a slight aroma of leather.

2009 Negramaro del Salento, Pietraluna, Racemi, Puglia, Italy, 13% abv
Real Wine Co, £6.99

The heel of Italy is a good place to go hunting for brawny reds at a fair price, and the local grape varieties do it best. Negramaro means 'the bitter black grape' but this wine is neither bitter nor black. Certainly the dark fruit is quite rough-cut but it's also scented with apple blossom, and the flavour is a friendly jumble of juicy plums and cherries knocking around with the peeled skin of ripe apples and pears.

2007 Tempranillo-Shiraz, Vino de la Tierra de Castilla y León, Storks' Tower, Antonio Barceló, Spain, 13.5% abv
Booths, Tesco, £6.99

Good chunky, muscular red. You don't normally see these two grapes blended together, but it works. The wine's reasonably tannic and quite peppery but that's well matched by good ripe black fruit and a welcome touch of savoury scent.

2009 Shiraz, Six Hats, Fairtrade, Western Cape, South Africa, 14% abv Asda, £6.97

For Fairtrade to succeed, it must ensure that the wine is good enough to command the slightly premium price we pay. Six Hats is doing that and I'm delighted to see Asda supporting Fairtrade wine by stocking this soft, lush red, with its flavour of smoky chocolate wafers and caramel, and its ripe black plum fruit.

• Six Hats Cabernet Sauvignon (Booths, £6.99) is also very good.

2008 Syrah-Merlot, Vin de Pays d'Oc, Reserve de l'Aube, Père Anselme, Languedoc-Roussillon, France, 13% abv
From Vineyards Direct, £6.95

You wouldn't normally blend the rich scented Syrah with the softer, milder Merlot – but this works. The wine is very warm and round, positively lush in its spiced plum sauce and stewed cherry way, but there's a bit of tannin there too and it all makes for a good, self-indulgent red.

AROUND £6

We've had a section focusing on wines below a fiver, or around a fiver, for some time now. The sheer unpredictability of government taxation policy has made pricing a nightmare for supermarkets and independent merchants alike, but, looking back over the last two years, the number of tax and duty rises is unprecedented. Even so, around a fiver is what a lot of us are prepared to pay for our 'supper wines', so what I've done this year is to call the section 'around six quid', but I've concentrated on wines at five pounds something and, when possible, four pounds something. When the wines go over six pounds, they're classy efforts that justify the extra money – but only when you're in the mood to spend it.

• In this section you will find white wines first, then reds, in descending price order.

WHITE WINE

2009 Chenin Blanc, Bush Vine, Zalze, Kleine Zalze, Coastal Region, South Africa, 14% abv
Waitrose, £6.49

Kleine Zalze is a relatively new, up-and-coming winery, which has delved back into South Africa's vine history and found plantings of old bush vines. Old Chenin vines are one of the Cape's treasures – as can be seen from the quality they can give. This wine smells of honey and bush grass and tastes of lemon pith, green apple pips and mineral dust, as well as honey drizzled over white melon. In a few years' time this will deepen to a marvellous flavour of custard and mandarin orange.

2008 Muscadet, Côtes de Grandlieu Sur Lie, Fief Guérin, Loire Valley, France, 12% abv
Waitrose, £6.49

It really is time Muscadet made a comeback. People who don't like Sauvignon Blanc and are tired of Chardonnay cast about for something gentle yet refreshing and all too often end up with an uninspiring Pinot Grigio. If you want bone dry but soft-centred white, modern Muscadet is a much better bet. This has a breezy, springtime smell of apple and pear blossom, soft ripe apple fruit cut through with a pebbly dryness, and finishes with a savoury creaminess from the months the wine has spent sitting on its yeast lees waiting to be bottled.

• There's quite a lot of good Muscadet around at the moment. Waitrose has another one, Champteloup, at £5.99; Sainsbury's Taste The Difference (£6.29) is made by the good Domaine Douillard; Morrison's tasty Domaine du Bois-Malinge is £5.99.

2008 Grillo, Italia, Sicily, Italy, 13.5% abv
Morrisons, £6.49, Waitrose, £6.79

Sicily is proving itself to be a 21st-century star performer at all levels.
It's not easy to make attractive whites in the boiling heat, but this is
very nice stuff, with an interesting flavour as though you'd somehow made a syrup out of rocks and apples
mashed together – and then you'd wrapped warm pastry round it!

2009 Chardonnay, Vredenhof Cellar Reserve, Western Cape, South Africa, 14% abv
Waitrose, £5.99

The kind of wine to give Chardonnay a good name again. I know a lot
of you simply won't drink £5.99 Chardonnay any more – but that's
because of all those sweetened-up, claggy Californian and Australian
brands. This is different. The oaky vanilla flavour is very subtly done;
the wine is quite rich, but that isn't sugar-richness, it's good-quality ripe fruit giving a delightful gentle
flavour of melon and peach slightly scented from the orchard, and allowing a subtle veil of dry mineral dust
to drift across the surface of the wine.

2009 Riesling, Cono Sur, Bío Bío Valley, Chile, 13.5% abv Tesco, £5.99

Riesling is a world-class grape variety capable of making every style of wine, from raspingly dry to startlingly
sweet. Chile is a newcomer to the Riesling game, using cool, damp
vineyards in the far south, and is rapidly making a reputation for this
style of Riesling – very light, mild, with delicate apple fruit and lemon
acid, a fragile floral scent, and a softness like sprinkled icing sugar,
leaving the wine not quite dry.

2009 Sauvignon Blanc, Silver Coast (Cave des Hauts de Gironde), Vin de France, 10% abv Booths, £5.99

'Naturally lighter' proclaims the label: it's only 10% alcohol. Hmm. Will it taste any good? Luckily it comes from one of the best producers of Sauvignon in all of Bordeaux and it tastes very good, managing to be zesty and fresh and weighty at the same time – blossom scent, ripe green apple, lemon zest and blackcurrant leaf – all at 10%.

• Bordeaux Blanc is a much underrated wine style. At around £6, the white is consistently better than Bordeaux red; it's also one of France's most attractive snappy white wines. If you don't have a Booths near you, Co-op (£5.89), Sainsbury's (£5.79), Tesco (£5.49) and Waitrose (£5.99) have the very tasty Calvet Limited Release Sauvignon Blanc, and M&S has a nice tangy Bordeaux Sauvignon Blanc (£6.49).

2009 Sauvignon Blanc, Vin de Pays du Val de Loire, France, 12% abv
Marks & Spencer, £5.99

Very attractive fresh, tangy Sauvignon. It's relatively soft in texture, but definitely sharp and leafy green in its flavours and pinging with juicy green apple fruit.

2009 The Society's Chilean Sauvignon Blanc, Leyda Valley, Chile, 13.5% abv
Wine Society, £5.95

The Wine Society clearly has excellent contacts in the Leyda Valley, because this is now one of Chile's trendier wine areas, and prices are on the rise – except at the Wine Society. It's the thrilling green tangy flavours that make Leyda Sauvignon so sought after: this is bursting with nettles, blackcurrant leaves, green peppers and green apples. My only carp is that the 2009 vintage seems slightly less dry than before. I hope that's a temporary blip, because fruit flavours like these don't need any help with sugar.

2008 Nico, Vinho Regional Terras do Sado, Pegões co-op, Setúbal Peninsula, Portugal, 10% abv
Booths, £5.49

This is a bit of an oddball – but I like it. It's not quite dry, and has a slightly grapy, muscaty quality, and yet is fresh and spritzy and full of verve. Rather an attractive grapefruit flower aroma mingles with the crunchiness of fresh green muscatel grapes and the prickle on your palate keeps it fresh.

2008 Vin de Pays du Gers, Pujalet, South-West France, 11.5% abv
Waitrose, £4.99

Very citrus, yet fleshy at the same time. It's like a sort of smoothie of grapefruit flesh and apple flesh that really revives the jaded palate, but you then get a slightly raspy edge like lemon pith and grapefruit pith zipping through the wine, to add just a slight, appetizing streak of bitterness to the experience.

2008 Harmonie de Gascogne, Vin de Pays des Côtes de Gascogne, Domaine de Pellehaut, South-West France, 12% abv
Booths, £4.99

A whole horde of different grape varieties go into this crowd-pleaser, but the ones that add most zing are the Colombard and the Sauvignon Blanc. They give the mouthwatering lemon zest and apple peel snap that really does make you salivate, while the other grapes fill out the palate and round out the texture.

2009 Saluti Bianco, Vino da Tavola, Italy, 12.5% abv
Waitrose, £4.99

This is 70% Sicilian Grecanico and Catarratto – both rather good grapes – along with 30% Trebbiano, one of Italy's most neutral varieties. The result's pretty good, not at all 'in yer face' – Italian whites rarely are – but delightfully scented with jasmine and the open slopes of the mountainside in summer. Refreshingly tart acid runs through the flavour, and the final effect is of soft, expensive leather.

RED WINE

2004 Langhe, Suagnà, Bricco Rosso, Piedmont, Italy, 13.5% abv
Wine Society, £6.50

Fascinating stuff. You don't get many Piedmont reds at this kind of price, and you certainly don't get many that are so easy to like. This tries to be a traditionally grumpy Piedmont brooder but can't pull it off because the fruit, despite being pretty dry, is marked by ripe black cherries and black plums, the acidity is cranberry juice run over stones, and there's a soft cushion of honey and cream in case the stones begin to intrude too much.

2009 Malbec, Fairtrade, Organic, Argentine Reserva (La Riojana co-op), Famatina Valley, La Rioja, Argentina, 13.5% abv
Co-op, £6.49

Lovely, lush red wine and, remember, every time you buy a bottle you're helping some really poor people have a better life. I've visited their villages and the Fairtrade premium has made a massive difference to their lives. Not only that: when you buy Fairtrade from the Co-op, they double the premium paid. Thank you Co-op. But the wine still has to be good – and this is a delight. Really hedonistic stuff with a scent of flowers and rosehip, juicy red fruit like a pie made of stewed red cherries and plums, topped with confectioners' cream and sprinkled with chocolate flakes.

2009 Shiraz-Merlot, Fairhills, Western Cape, South Africa, 14% abv
Morrisons, £6.49

Fairhills has become an important Fairtrade brand and this one delivers on taste. Some Cape reds can be a bit too rough and ready, but although this one is quite chewy, it has more than enough fruit to balance out any toughness and the effect is more of ripe dark fruit and chocolate than anything bitter.

2008 Nero d'Avola-Syrah, AgroGento, Sicily, Italy, 13% abv
Playford Ros, £6.44

This is a very modern marriage between two ancient grape varieties, and it's only fitting that the ceremony should take place in Sicily, where old meets new like almost nowhere else in Europe. Syrah is the interloper, but just might be related to Nero d'Avola after some grapy tryst lost in the mists of time. They both grow very well here and this is delightful wine, smelling of marzipan and violets and tasting of black plums and cherries made attractively chewy by a little skinsy tannin.

2009 Côtes du Ventoux, La Vieille Ferme, Rhône Valley, France, 13.5% abv
Waitrose, £6.39

This wine comes from the slopes of Mont Ventoux, on the eastern side of the Rhône Valley, and it's made by a bunch of guys most famous for the Châteauneuf-du-Pape Château de Beaucastel. The cool mountain fruit marries well with the beefy aspirations of the winemakers, because this is rich, jammy red wine with a really ripe fruit feel and some nutty creamy fatness, yet it

stays fresh, and is given an appetizing dryness by a swish of sun-soaked hillside herbs.

• La Vieille Ferme Côtes du Lubéron (white, £6.39) is equally good.

2009 Shiraz, DB Family Selection, De Bortoli, South Eastern Australia, 14% abv
Waitrose, £6.29

De Bortoli are best known in the red wine world for their delicate, charming Pinot Noirs, but I sometimes think that their heart is more in the Shiraz camp, because at all price levels and in all styles, beefy to fragrant, they do Shiraz very well. This is pretty rich – full of black plum syrup and licorice, anise, herbs and kitchen spice. Full, rich, warm, sun-kissed stuff.

2009 Beaujolais-Villages, France, 12.5% abv Tesco, £5.99

If only the regular run of Beaujolais were this good, and at this price, maybe we'd all start drinking it again. The real Beaujolais is France's juiciest, most come-hither, gurgle-it-down red. We really need to rediscover it. The wine isn't oaky, it's usually fairly low in alcohol and it's bursting with fresh optimistic fruit. This one's a belter – almost more rich fruit than you're ready for – piles of juicy, slightly bruised strawberry and peach all tumbled together and a nice earthy rub to keep it refreshing.

2009 Cabernet Sauvignon, Douglas Green, Western Cape, South Africa, 14% abv Morrisons, £5.99

Good, deep, dark red with lots of fruit. Some South African Cabernets can taste too earthy and rough, but this one, despite being pretty solid, has a good wodge of chunky fruit at its heart, a bit of leafy freshness and an attractively sun-baked dust and creamy texture.

2008 Côtes du Rhône-Villages Reserve (Du Peloux), Rhône Valley, France, 13.5% abv
Tesco, £5.99

This absolutely hits the spot – bang in the middle of that rich ripe red herb-splashed fruit that makes the Rhône rock. It's not massive or dense, though it is serious – there's a perfectly welcome tannic nip to the wine – but it's the fruit and herbs that do it for me: honey-flecked strawberry fruit veering towards something darker, like loganberry, and with a few chunks of licorice and black chocolate dropped into the vat, a memory of southern heat, a vague suggestion of raisins and dates, and the whole thing run over rocks and sunshine with the wild herbs of the garrigue.

2008 Garnacha, Borsao, Campo de Borja, Spain, 13.5% abv
D Byrne, Oxford Wine Company, Reserve Wines, WoodWinters and other independents, £5.99

The Garnacha grape is the most widely planted black grape in the world, and a good deal of it sprawls over the hot hinterland of north-eastern Spain, where until recently, frankly, it went to waste. But an influx of new winemakers – including Aussies and Brits – now means that the sight of the name 'Garnacha' on a label should make any red-blooded winedrinker's heart beat a little faster. This is juicy but powerful, sturdy yet with loads of red cherry and red plum fruit, scented with dried sage, finished off with the fruit rolled in rock dust.

2008 Nero d'Avola, Terre dell'Isola, Sicily, Italy, 13% abv
Majestic, £5.99

Nero d'Avola is such a good grape – it can do anything from bright juicy gluggers to powerful world-class heavyweights, yet it never loses the fundamental joy of the dark sweet fruit at its core. This one's on the lighter side, to quaff, not to ponder over, but it still offers marvellous mellow dark juicy fruit couched in good-natured language.

2009 Syrah, Ardèche, Vignerons Ardéchois, Rhône Valley, France, 12.5% abv
Christopher Piper Wines, £5.80

Lovely stuff. The Ardèche is virtually next door to really good Rhône Valley areas like St-Joseph, and the Syrah clearly flourishes there. The lovely thing about Ardèche Syrah is that it isn't tarted up and smothered with expensive new oak. And it turns out like this – scented, floral, with a beautiful chubby texture of crème fraîche, fat plums and rosehips tempered by a bit of tannin, and promising a beguiling whiff of perfumed leather by Christmas.

2008 Rioja, Vega Ariana, Spain, 14% abv
Waitrose, £5.69

Affordable Rioja that tastes like the gorgeous old styles we all fell in love with way back when. Ah, bliss. A lot of modern Rioja seems too desperate to be taken awfully seriously, yet it was the lovely, mellow 'red wine without tears' flavour of Rioja that we were all seduced by. And here it is – bruised squashy strawberries, gradually opening out into a richer broader flavour of honey and cream, a bit of peach, a flicker of stones, and lots more squashy red fruit.

2003 Viña Decana Reserva, Utiel Requena, Valencia, Spain, 13% abv
Aldi, £4.99

This is a great mishmash of French and Spanish grape varieties from Spain's boiling south, and it's a success. Part of the wine seems to want to be an old-style Rioja – rich fudge and vanilla oak – yet part of it is more like modern Bordeaux – solid, dark plum fruit, chewy tannin, but still fresh. An unlikely marriage, but it works here.

2007 Dão, Portugal, 13% abv
Tesco, £4.79

It's hard enough to find a delicious expensive Dão in our High Streets, let alone an absolute stonker for less than a fiver. Dão is quite possibly Portugal's most serious wine region and it specializes in pretty damn serious red wines. Well, I suppose this *is* serious. It's blackish in colour, has some of the warm scent of flowers gasping for moisture on a south-facing wall, and a rocky, mineral texture to get your teeth into. Yet it's also relatively soft, and exudes dark loganberry, mulberry and plum fruit. Top stuff.

2009 Gran López, Campo de Borja (Santo Cristo co-op), Aragón, Spain, 14% abv Waitrose, £4.79

A mix of Spain's two leading black grape varieties, Garnacha and Tempranillo, from Campo de Borja, which is one of Europe's best bargain centres for red wine. This is soft and full, mixing the bright crispness of fresh eating apples with the softer red fruit of strawberries. A hint of herbs and a slightly stony dryness combine with a touch of tannin to create a really good suppertime red.

2009 Pinotage (Swartland Winery), South Africa, 14% abv Tesco, £4.79

Pinotage is a grape with a reputation for being a bit of a beast. But Pinotage is also a grape that revels in being tamed and it rewards the tamer with delightful scent. This is made at Swartland Winery, a big

operation where they clearly enjoy cracking the whip, because this is full and juicy and balanced, not aggressive, with that typically tasty Pinotage mix of mulberry fruit, fluffy apple flesh acidity and toasted marshmallow soft centre just kept in line by a sniff of black pepper and tree bark.

2009 Tempranillo, Sabina, Navarra, Spain, 13% abv Wine Society, £4.75

Tempranillo means the early grape – early to ripen, and, frankly, often at its best drunk early too. I know Tempranillo makes the grand long-lasting reds of Rioja and Ribera del Duero, but it's also brilliantly suited to what the Spanish call *joven* – young wine. This is a good example. It's bursting with exuberant raspberry and red plum fruit, both bright yet stewy at the same time – think of your mum's fruit pies when you were a kid – but it also has a quite stern streak of tannin, a bit like a popular schoolmaster keeping discipline in an end-of-term classroom.

CHEAP AND CHEERFUL

There was a time earlier this year when I really thought there would be no point in trying to do a cheap and cheerful section – surely all the decent cheap stuff would have risen in price too much with the welter of different tax and duty rises this year has seen. Couple that with our utterly feeble currency and the whole thing looked like a lost cause. But then I started tasting around, and, although there are far fewer drinkable wines around the £3 mark – as in, almost none – there are still quite a few decent drops nearer £4, especially when you look in unfashionable places like Hungary or parts of southern France. There are also places that have grown too many grapes and need to offload before the new vintage – you'll see Australia, South Africa and South America featuring here. So we can still drink well at the bottom of the price scale, but it's getting harder all the time.

• In this section you will find white wines first, then reds, in descending price order.

WHITE WINE

2008 Cserszegi Füszeres, Hilltop Tradition, Neszmély, Hungary, 11% abv
Morrisons, £4.29

I think you pronounce this 'sher… chersh' – oh, never mind; it's the unpronounceable one in the Hungarian section. Actually, that won't help. The country's tourist publicity literature boasts that Hungarian is the second most difficult language in the world. What's the most difficult, for goodness sake? Well, if you like grapefruit marmalade and lime marmalade with all their acidity and fruit and zesty chunks of peel, and if you like musky, floral scents – all that in a bright fresh wine, and only 11% alcohol – pluck up your courage and grab a bottle of this off the shelf.

2009 Australian Chardonnay, South Australia, 12.5% abv
Asda, £3.99

Pretty good basic Aussie Chardie, with a bit more personality and a bit less sugar than most. Mild but tasty, soft apple and greengage fruit sharpened up by just a touch of grapefuit, and there's a flicker of smoky spice hanging in there.

2009 Cuvée Pêcheur, Comté Tolosan, South-West France, 11.5% abv
Waitrose, £3.99

Every year, Cuvée Pêcheur delivers – bright, fresh, tasty, doing the tangy Sauvignon job for a couple of quid less. This positively bounces off your tongue, a trampoline of lemon zest, apple peel and summer country dust.
• The red Cuvée Chasseur (£3.99) is also good.

2009 Eva's Vineyard, Hilltop Estate, Neszmély, Hungary, 12% abv Waitrose, £3.99

Hungary is such a good grape-growing country, and yet they find it virtually impossible to persuade us to pay a proper price for their wines. While I'm sympathetic to the producers, the least we can do is lap up the classy, low-priced delights hitting our shores. This is a three-variety blend from the excellent Neszmély winery: it's bright, balanced, elegant, fresh, lemon zest sharpening up eating apple peel and a whiff of some indistinct, frail, cold springtime scent.

House Muscadet (Lacheteau), Loire Valley, France, 12% abv
Sainsbury's, £3.99

'House' is a pretty simple concept developed by Sainsbury's. We've all asked for 'house' red or white in a bar or restaurant. It's the basic choice but the proprietor is supposed to be proud of it. Well, next time you're in Sainsbury's, check out their new 'house' range. I think this Muscadet is just right for a 'house' white – fresh, bright, balanced, bone-dry, a touch of attractive creamy softness and a hint of prickle in the palate.

2009 Marsanne, Pays d'Oc (Domaine de Corneille), Languedoc-Roussillon, France, 12.5% abv
Asda, £3.98

Really nice full-bodied white from a single estate at a more than fair price. Marsanne gives fat, waxy wines with a flicker of honeysuckle, and this one mixes the honeysuckle scent with an appleyness that is almost as rich as apple purée yet cut through with the zesty acidity of boiled lemons. It is dry, but is rich enough to seem off-dry.

RED WINE

2009 Gamay, Vin de Pays de l'Ardèche (Cave de St-Désirat), Rhône Valley, France, 12% abv
Marks & Spencer, £4.29

This is the best red party glugger on the market. I'm throwing down the gauntlet. Find me a better bright, breezy, fruity, friendly glass of ripper red than this. The guys who make it are actually pretty serious red Rhône producers, but this is like the Beaujolais of my dreams – strawberry, pear and peach fruit kept rough and ready by stones and minerals, pepper and apple peel. Ultimately it's all about the pleasure measure.

2009 Argentinian Malbec (Bodegas Trivento), Mendoza, Argentina, 13% abv
Asda, £4.24

Does the label really say 'Fab with chilli con carne'? Well, it's right. Chilli is a bit of a blaster for wine, but this bright red could handle it, with its floral perfume, crunchy damson and plum fruit and…what's that flavour? Putty? Snowcem paint? Or just a bit of Andes rock that's tumbled into the vat.

2008 Garnacha, Gran Tesoro (Bodegas Borsao), Campo de Borja, Aragón, Spain, 13.5% abv
Booths, Tesco, £3.99

This wine comes from old vines grown in the vast hinterland of north-eastern Spain. The vines sprawl all over the place – Spain does have more vines than any other country – largely because nothing else will grow there. They're old, they're good, but until recently they were totally wasted on rubbish winemaking. That's all changing and areas like this one, Campo de Borja, are now sources of lovely, crunchy, stewy (well, it *is* hot), strawberry-fruited reds, flecked with herbs and roughened up with the odd rock – but it's the rich gutsy red fruit that is at the heart of the wine.

House Shiraz, South Eastern Australia, 13.5% abv
Sainsbury's, £3.99

Here's my pick of the 'house' reds from Sainsbury's new range. Sainsbury's has always had a good, gutsy, affordable Aussie Shiraz, and this one's no exception. It's full, it's juicy, it's got rich, chunky blackberry fruit, a decent whiff of spice, and a chewy edge to make it appetizing and more-ish.
• The House Valpolicella (£3.79) is a bright, juicy glugger and only 11.5% alcohol; the House Rioja, Torla (£3.99) is unoaked, perfumed and fruity.

2009 Trinacria, Rosso, Sicily, Italy, 12% abv
Waitrose, £3.99

Sicily is really proving itself at every level of winemaking. There are some superb high-end expensive reds and whites, but quaffers haven't been neglected. Being

so far south, almost in Africa, you'd expect Sicilian reds to be baked, but they have a range of fabulous, heat-resistant black grapes – this wine uses Nero d'Avola, Frappato and Nerello – as well as some seriously good and surprisingly cool vineyards. The result is this – bright, almost jelly baby, fruit gum drinkability, juicy raspberry fruit and quite adult tannin and acidity. And it's only 12% alcohol.

2008 Tempranillo, Utiel Requena, Toro Loco, Valencia, Spain, 12.5% abv
Aldi, £3.49

It is really tough to keep any fresh flavour in the wine in Utiel Requena, a devil's cauldron of a place in south-east Spain which used to be famous for making a thick, blackstrap wine sent off all over Europe to beef up feebler brews. But there's been a revolution down there. You can still just about taste some heat-shrivelled raisins, but mostly it's bright, crunchy, strawberry and raspberry fruit, a hint of apple blossom scent, and some rock dust minerals.

2009 Chilean Cabernet Sauvignon, Valle Central, Chile, 13% abv
Asda, £3.11

Asda has had good cheap Chileans for some years now, but they've never been better value than this. This is pretty dark for a cheap red, with good loganberry fruit along with red plum and a hint of blackcurrant. But it's juicy, not rough, and seriously good at this price.

ROSÉ WINES

I was very encouraged by the Champions League football final this year. Not because of the football, but because a bunch of lads in my street were having a football party and I watched them lug slabs of beer and cases of potato crisps into their house – and then two of the beefiest blokes brought up the rear with armfuls of wine. Not red, not white. Pink. And it wasn't sweet slop. It was French dry rosé. Real wine, but pink. There really is a rosé revolution going on when the football crowd embraces it. And the statisticians. The Office for National Statistics uses a 'shopping basket' to calculate inflation. The items it includes are reckoned to reflect our nation's buying habits. This year they added rosé wine for the first time (and took out boxed wine, praise be). With us more than doubling our rosé drinking in the last five years, and no sign of the trend reversing, here's my choice for the year.

• The wines are listed in descending price order.

2009 Dão, Touriga Nacional Rosé, Quinta da Falorca, Quinta Vale das Escadinhas, Portugal, 13.5% abv

Armit, £11.30

Touriga Nacional is Portugal's most serious red grape variety and Dão is pretty much the country's most serious red wine region. But everyone has to let their hair down now and then. Even so, there's a vaguely austere disciplinarian feeling to this wine – dry, weighty, flowing over stones, but the apple flesh fruit is ripe and gentle and the final effect is well-behaved but refreshing.

2009 English Rosé, Chapel Down, Kent, England, 12% abv

Marks & Spencer, £10.99

Chapel Down is based in Kent, but draws its fruit from right across south-east England. This shows in the amazing array of grape varieties in this wine: Pinot Noir dominates, but it's only a third; English speciality red varieties Rondo and Regent add a third more; but then it's everything from the hedgerow – scented Bacchus, Schönburger, Huxelrebe, Pinot Gris, Chardonnay – thrown into the vat. Even a small amount of aromatic Bacchus adds a lovely, bright elderflower scent to a full, rather stony, reasonably acid pink that ends up quintessentially stiff upper lip English just hinting at a wink and a smile.

2009 Somontano, Tempranillo-Cabernet Sauvignon, Bestué, Otto Bestué, Spain, 13.5% abv

Adnams, £9.50; Great Western Wine, £9.95

The bright pink-red colour will warn you that this isn't subtle. It's pretty full-bodied, rather serious wine that happens to be dark pink. It has an almost syrupy weight, but it's an attractive strawberry syrup, and is offset by a positively white-wine snappy acidity and very endearing apple and pear flesh fruit. Quite a mouthful, but a good one.

2009 Côtes de Provence, Château Saint Baillon, Provence, France, 13% abv
Goedhuis, £9.01

Provence rosés sometimes seem to compete with each other to exhibit the least colour possible – and to have the least flavour possible, for that matter. But there is something about their illusory tinge of pink and their soothing texture that makes the best ones positively beguiling. This is limpid, filigree, nebulous, diaphanous, like a smear of face cream on a boudoir looking glass. Its flavours are fluffy, insubstantial, a hint of anise, a Golden Delicious sliced wafer-thin and rubbed with Havana tobacco, a texture like spring water trickling over your tongue.

2009 Coteaux d'Aix-en-Provence Rosé, La Chapelle, Château Pigoudet, Provence, France, 13.5% abv
Majestic, £8.99

People have been hailing Coteaux d'Aix-en-Provence as the next big southern French thing ever since Queen Victoria was a boy. Yet it hasn't happened. And she wasn't. But there are a few properties that turn out serious pinks and reds, not just tourist fodder. Pigoudet is one: it makes a big, balanced red, and this rather statuesque rosé – almost stony, yet with an invigorating cold pink fruit and a soft creamy finish.

2009 Rosé de la Chevalière, Vin de Pays d'Oc, Mas la Chevalière/Laroche, Languedoc, France, 12% abv
Flying Corkscrew, Liberty Wines, £8.99

Laroche is a Chablis expert, but years ago Michel Laroche felt constricted by the tight rules in Chablis and wanted to experiment, so he headed for the Languedoc. Along with good reds and whites, he makes this gently fruity pink with flavours of apple, pear and strawberry and a refreshing lick of lemon acidity.

2009 Coteaux du Languedoc Rosé, Les Arbousiers, Languedoc, France, 12.5% abv
Virgin Wines, £7.49

This comes from the good red wine village of Montpeyroux – and although it's lovely and fresh now, it has the pedigree to age for a year if you want. Right now it's blossomy bright, with pink apple and peach flesh fruit but dry and cut with lemon juice. A touch of chocolate will appear in the mix if you age it.

2009 Pinot Rosé, Pays d'Oc, Domaine Begude, Languedoc, France, 11.5% abv
Majestic, £7.49

Pinot Noir rosés are some of the most expensive in France – usually from Burgundy or places like Sancerre – and they're often disappointing. So, save a bit of money and head south-west to Limoux, where Domaine Begude majors on a highly regarded Chardonnay, but finds time for this delightful fresh yet full-bodied pink, with the bite of ripe apple peel and the mild fruitiness of strawberry. And it's bone dry.

2009 Rosé, Boschendal, Coastal Region, South Africa, 13% abv
Majestic, £7.49; Co-op, £6.49

Here's something slightly chubby and pink of cheek. It's fairly dry, despite its reassuring rounded texture, and offers fresh strawberry fruit and pear and apple flesh to go with its glyceriny texture.

2009 Merlot-Cabernet Sauvignon, Liboreau, Vin de Pays Charentais, France, 12.5% abv
Laithwaites, £6.99

This comes from the Cognac region of France. White grapes struggle to ripen there, let alone red, but when the sun shines, as it did in 2009, they can make some delightful rosés, with a serious texture helped by the leafy greenness in the fruit, a stony dryness and gentle apple and strawberry fruit soothed slightly with cream.

NV House Zinfandel Rosé, USA, 10% abv
Sainsbury's, £4.29

Most people don't have the slightest idea what proper Zinfandel pink should taste like since there's so much sugar-water on the market. Well, it should taste like this. It's certainly not dry, but it's not cloying, and with a flavour of grapeskin and brambles and tobacco. All it needs is a real good chilling before you drink it.

2008 Toro Loco Rosé, Utiel Requena, Valencia, Spain, 12% abv
Aldi, £3.49

Utiel Requena is a broiling part of Spain; I've always been amazed when anything not tasting of raisins emerged. But that's to underestimate the Bobal grape. It's spent centuries out in the arid fields working out how to cope with the heat, and a new wave of winemakers is coaxing surprisingly fresh flavours from it. This has been picked early and manages to blend the high summeriness of hot, baked stones with good apple peel acidity, strawberry fruit gum, and a drizzle of icing sugar.

Keeping it light

We're becoming increasingly disenchanted with high-alcohol wines. So, increasingly, I'm checking the alcohol content of the wines I recommend. Here are my suggestions for drinks with fab flavours that won't leave you fuzzy-headed the next morning.

More and more wines seem to be hitting our shores at 14.5%, 15% – a couple of wines in this year's tastings came in at 15.5%. That's fine if the alcohol is balanced by ripe fruit and good acidity – but don't think of these wines as a jolly beverage to knock back with your lamb chops: you'll be asleep or drunk before you've got the meat off the barbie.

Now, some wines have traditionally been high in alcohol, and wear their strength well, but there are far too many wines that – less than a decade ago – used to perform at 11.5–12.5% alcohol and which are now adding at least a degree – and often more – to their strength, seemingly in an effort to ape the ripe round flavours of the New World. Thank goodness there are still a significant number showing more restraint.

At 12.5% there are lots of wines, particularly from cooler parts of France – most Beaujolais is 12–12.5% – northern Italy, where the most famous examples would be the Veneto reds Valpolicella and Bardolino and the white Soave, and from numerous parts of Eastern Europe, particularly Hungary.

But we've set the bar at 12%. This cuts out a lot of red wines; the slightly tart, refreshing white styles that sit easily at 12% can develop better flavour at a lower strength than most reds can. This exercise reminded us that Germany is full of fantastic Riesling wines as low as 8%. Muscadet is usually only 12%. Most supermarket house reds and whites are 11.5–12%. Western Australian whites are often 12%. And Champagne, along with most other sparkling wines, is only 12%. Hallelujah.

• VdP = Vin de Pays

White wine

- 2009 Airén-Sauvignon Blanc, Gran López, La Mancha, Spain, £4.79, Waitrose, 11.5% abv
- 2009 Bacchus, Chapel Down, Kent, England, c.£10, Majestic, Waitrose, 12% abv
- 2008 Bordeaux Blanc Sec, Pezat, Ch. Teyssier, France, £9, Big Red Wine Co, 12% abv
- 2009 Bordeaux Sauvignon Blanc, Calvet Limited Release, France, £6–8, Co-op, Sainsbury's, Tesco, Waitrose, 12% abv
- 2009 Bordeaux Sauvignon-Sémillon, Château La Freynelle, France, £8–£9, Oxford Wine Co, Stainton Wines, 12% abv
- 2007 Chablis (La Chablisienne), Burgundy, France, £9.99, Marks & Spencer, 12% abv
- 2008 Chablis, 1er Cru Les Vaudevey, Dom. Laroche, Burgundy, France, £19.99, Liberty Wines, 12% abv
- 2008 Chardonnay Bourgogne, Jurassique, Jean-Marc Brocard, Burgundy, France, £8.99, Booths, 12% abv
- 2008 Chenin Blanc (cool-fermented), La Grille, Loire Valley, France, £6.99, Majestic, 11% abv
- 2010 Colombard, La Biondina, Primo Estate, McLaren Vale, South Australia, £8.99, AustralianWineCentre.co.uk, 12% abv
- 2008 Cserszegi Füszeres, Hilltop Tradition, Neszmély, Hungary, £4.29, Morrisons, 11% abv (page 98)
- 2009 Clair-ette de Roquefort, VdP des Bouches du Rhône, Dom. de Roquefort, £10.75, Lea & Sandeman, 12% abv
- 2009 Cullen, Margaret River White, Western Australia, £11.99, Booths, 12% abv
- 2009 Cuvée Pêcheur, Comté Tolosan, South-West France, £3.99, Waitrose, 11.5% abv (page 98)
- 2009 Cuvée de Richard, VdP du Comté Tolosan, South-West France, £4.49, Majestic, 11.5% abv

- NV VdP des Côtes de Gascogne, South-West France, £3.99, Sainsbury's, 11.5% abv
- 2008 VdP des Côtes de Gascogne, Harmonie de Gascogne, Domaine de Pellehaut, South-West France, £4.99, Booths, 12% abv (page 88)
- 2009 VdP des Côtes de Gascogne, Domaine de Plantérieu, South-West France, £5.49, Waitrose, 10.5% abv
- 2009 VdP du Gers, Lesc, Producteurs Plaimont, South-West France, £6.49, Les Caves de Pyrène, 11.5% abv
- 2008 VdP du Gers, Pujalet, South-West France, £4.99, Waitrose, 11.5% abv (page 88)
- 2009 Eva's Vineyard, Hilltop Estate, Neszmély, Hungary, £3.99, Waitrose, 12% abv (page 99)
- 2009 (Spanish) Macabeo, Cariñena, Spain, £4.29, Marks & Spencer, 12% abv
- 2008 Muscadet Côtes de Grandlieu sur lie, Fief Guérin, Loire Valley, France, £6.49, Waitrose, 12% abv (page 84)
- NV Muscadet (House), Loire Valley, France, £3.99, Sainsbury's, 12% abv (page 99)
- 2009 Muscadet Sèvre et Maine, Domaine du Bois-Malinge, Loire Valley, France, £5.99, Morrisons, 12% abv
- 2009 Muscadet Sèvre et Maine sur lie, Taste the Difference (Domaine Douillard), Loire Valley, France, £6.29, Sainsbury's, 12% abv
- 2008 Nico, Vinho Regional Terras do Sado, Pegões co-op, Setúbal Peninsula, Portugal, £5.49, Booths, 10% abv (page 87)
- 2009 Petit Chablis, Laroche, Burgundy, France, £12.99, Flying Corkscrew, Liberty Wines, 11.5% abv
- Pinot Grigio, Budavar, Hungary, £3.59, Aldi, 11.5% abv
- 2009 Pinot Grigio, Heartland Wines, Langhorne Creek-Limestone Coast, South Australia, £10.95, Great Western Wine, 12% abv

- 2008 Riesling, Tim Adams, Clare Valley, South Australia, £9.29, Tesco, 11.5% abv (page 28)
- 2008 Riesling, Bassermann-Jordan, Pfalz, Germany, £8.99, Waitrose, 10% abv (page 26)
- 2009 Riesling, The Doctor's, Forrest Estate, Marlborough, New Zealand, £8.99, Adnams, 8.5% abv
- 2009 Riesling, Eldredge, Clare Valley, South Australia, £9.99, Oz Wines, 12% abv
- 2009 Riesling, Dr L, Loosen, Mosel, Germany, £7–8, widely available, 8.5% abv
- 2009 Riesling, Magnus, Leasingham Wines, Clare Valley, South Australia, c.£8.25, Sainsbury's and others, 12% abv
- 2009 Riesling, Opou Vineyard, Millton, Gisborne, New Zealand, £11.75, Vintage Roots, 12% abv
- 2008 Riesling, Te Muna Road, Craggy Range, Martinborough, New Zealand, £12.95, Wine Society, 11.7% abv
- 2009 Riesling, Tingleup Vineyard, Great Southern, Western Australia, £8.49, Tesco Finest, 12% abv (page 69)
- 2009 Riesling, Dr Wagner, Mosel, Germany, £7.99, Waitrose, 10% abv
- 2006 Riesling Spätlese, Kreuznacher Krötenpfuhl, Dönnhoff, Nahe, Germany, £18.99, Waitrose, 8% abv (page 58)
- 2005 Riesling Spätlese, Piesporter Goldtröpfchen, Reichsgraf von Kesselstatt, Mosel, Germany, £13.95, Wine Society, 8% abv
- 2009 Saumur, Les Andides, Loire Valley, France, £6.99, Waitrose, 12% abv
- 2009 Sauvignon Blanc, Champteloup, Touraine, Loire Valley, France, £7.49, Waitrose, 12% abv
- 2009 Sauvignon Blanc, VdP Charentais, Dom. Gardrat, France, £8.50, Yapp Brothers, 11.5% abv (page 68)
- 2009 Sauvignon Blanc, Jacques Lurton Selection, VdP du Val de Loire, France, £4.99, Sainsbury's, 11.5% abv
- 2009 Sauvignon Blanc, Lobster Reef, Cape Campbell, Marlborough, New Zealand, £8.99, Oddbins, 12% abv
- 2009 Sauvignon Blanc, Silver Coast (Cave des Hauts de Gironde), France, £5.99, Booths, 10% abv (page 86)
- 2009 Sauvignon Blanc, Sincérité, VdP du Val de Loire, Joseph Mellot, France, £7.49, Averys, 12% abv
- 2009 Sauvignon Blanc, VdP du Val de Loire, France, £5.99, Marks & Spencer, 12% abv (page 86)
- 2009 Sauvignon Blanc-Gros Manseng, Les Montgolfiers, VdP des Côtes de Gascogne, South-West France, £6.99, Tesco, 12% abv
- 2008 Vin de Savoie, Chignin, Domaine Gilles Berlioz, France, £9.95, Wine Society, 11.5% abv (page 66)
- 2009 Savoie, L'Orangerie, P & F Tiollier, France, £8.95, Yapp Brothers, 11% abv
- 2006 Semillon, Denman Vineyard, Hunter Valley, New South Wales, Australia, £7.99, Tesco Finest, 10.5% abv
- 2008 Semillon, Peter Lehmann, Barossa, South Australia, £7.49, Oddbins, 10.5% abv
- 2004 Semillon, Margaret, Peter Lehmann, Barossa, South Australia, £14.50, Vin du Van, 11.5% abv (page 48)
- 2008 Semillon, Vasse Felix, Margaret River, Western Australia, £12.99, Marks & Spencer, 11.5% abv
- 2008 Semillon-Sauvignon Blanc, See Saw, South Australia, £7.99, Waitrose, 12% abv
- 2009 Soave, Pieropan, Veneto, Italy, c.£12, Booths, Colchester Wine, Jeroboams, Lea & Sandeman, Liberty Wines, Philglas & Swiggot, Valvona & Crolla, WoodWinters, Wright Wine Co, 12% abv (page 37)
- 2009 Soave Classico, Veneto, Italy, £5.98, Asda Extra Special, 12% abv

- 2009 Trinacria Bianco, Sicily, Italy, £3.99, Waitrose, 12% abv
- 2009 Verdicchio dei Castelli di Jesi Classico, Castellani, Italy, £4.28, Asda, 12% abv
- 2009 Vieille Fontaine, VdP d'Oc, Languedoc-Roussillon, France, £3.99, Tesco, 11.5% abv
- 2009 Viña Esmeralda, Torres, Catalunya, Spain, c.£7.50, widely available, 11.5% abv
- 2009 Viña Sol, Torres, Catalunya, Spain, c.£6.50, widely available, 11.5% abv
- 2009 Vinho Verde, Quinta de Azevedo, Sogrape, Portugal, £6–7, Majestic, Waitrose, 11% abv (page 46)

Rosé wine

- 2009 Cuvée Fleur, Pays de l'Hérault, Languedoc-Roussillon, France, £4.29, Waitrose, 12% abv
- 2009 English Rosé (Chapel Down), £10.99, Marks & Spencer, 12% abv (page 104)
- VdP du Gard Rosé, Baron St-Jean, Languedoc, France, £3.29, Aldi, 12% abv
- 2009 Pinot Rosé, Pays d'Oc, Domaine Begude, Languedoc, France, £7.49, Majestic, 11.5% abv (page 106)
- 2009 VdP d'Oc, Rosé de la Chevalière, Laroche, Languedoc, France, £8.99, Flying Corkscrew, Liberty Wines, 12% abv (page 106)
- 2009 Utiel-Requena, Las Falleras Rosé, Valencia, Spain, £4.29, Marks & Spencer, 12% abv
- 2009 Utiel-Requena, Toro Loco Rosé, Valencia, Spain, £3.49, Aldi, 12% abv (page 107)
- 2009 Valencia, M de Murviedro Rosé, Spain, £5.83, Asda, 12% abv
- NV Zinfandel Rosé (House), USA, £4.29, Sainsbury's, 10% abv (page 107)

Red wine

- 2009 Cheverny, Clos du Tue-Boeuf, Loire Valley, France, £14.99, Les Caves de Pyrène, Oddbins, 12% abv (page 34)
- 2008 Côtes de Gascogne, Cuvée Spéciale, South-West France, £5.49, Marks & Spencer, 12% abv
- 2009 Côte Roannaise, Dom. Robert Sérol, Loire Valley, France, £8.85, Christopher Piper, 12% abv (page 39)
- 2009 Cuvée Chasseur, Pays de l'Hérault, Languedoc-Roussillon, France, £3.99, Waitrose, 12% abv
- 2009 Cuvée de Richard, VdP de l'Aude, Languedoc-Roussillon, France, £4.49, Majestic, 12% abv
- 2009 Gamay, VdP de l'Ardèche (Cave de St-Désirat), Rhône Valley, France, £4.29, Marks & Spencer, 12% abv (page 100)
- 2008 (Spanish) Garnacha-Shiraz, Cariñena, Spain, £4.29, Marks & Spencer, 12% abv
- 2008 Lambrusco dell'Emilia, Camillo Donati, Italy, £12.99, Les Caves de Pyrène, 12% abv (page 121)
- 2008 Le Rouge est mis, Vin de table, Thierry Puzelat, £16.99, Les Caves de Pyrène, 12% abv
- 2009 Trinacria Rosso, Sicily, Italy, £3.99, Waitrose, 12% abv (page 101)
- 2009 Valpolicella, Adalia, Veneto, Italy, £12.99, Oddbins, 12% abv
- Valpolicella (House), Veneto, Italy, £3.79, Sainsbury's, 11.5% abv

It's a tricky decision in the midst of an economic crisis and the great sword of cutbacks, retrenchment and redundancy hanging over the nation: do we drink fizz? Can we be seen to drink fizz? Must we do it in sinful secrecy? Well, what seems to have happened is that people still feel the need for some sparkle in their lives, but the ostentatious glugging of bling bling labels in public places seems to be disapproved of. Prosecco is booming – affordable, not ostentatious – New World fizzes are doing well. Some Champagne is selling but the big brands are finding it tough. What a surprise. As the crisis struck they all raised their prices. Thanks, fellas, nice of you. This year, after we understandably stopped buying their stuff, the tip top labels have been discounted by as much as 50%. So if you do want to drink a top label, wait until the supermarkets offload some, probably around Christmas time. If you're not a label drinker, the following wines are here because they taste good, not look smart.

• The wines are listed in descending price order.

2004 Champagne Blanc de Blancs Grand Cru, Le Mesnil, France, 12% abv
Waitrose, £30.99

Le Mesnil is my favourite village in all of Champagne. At the top of the little main street is one of France's smallest co-operatives. The sum total of vines? 25 hectares. But that's 25 hectares of some of the greatest vines in France. And the £30.99 you pay for this wine isn't shared with marketing men and advertising budgets and supermodels spilling it over themselves in nightclubs. Deduct the Chancellor's tithe, and you're spending the rest on sheer, gorgeous quality of grapes and careful, traditional winemaking by people who have Chardonnay in their lifeblood. This is still fresh and young, and ideally wants another two or three years to stun you with its quality, but the balance is perfect, the fresh apple fruit combines beautifully with yeasty cream, honey bread and the savoury softness of porridge oats.

NV Champagne Brut Réserve, Charles Heidsieck, France, 12% abv
Waitrose and others, £30.99

Charles Heidsieck is a big Champagne company that has decided that the best way to ensure profitability is to make a supremely good product which then basically sells itself. When was the last time you saw a

Charles Heidsieck advertisement? I can't recall any. That's millions saved for a start. This still tastes quite young, but 40% of the wine is 'reserve' wine, with an average age of eight years, which immeasurably improves the texture and flavour of the wine. This is a foaming delight, its cascade of bubbles carrying a gorgeous scented chocolate cream richness, oatmeal roundness and bright, appetizing ripe apple acid.

NV Champagne, Esprit Brut, Henri Giraud, France, 12% abv
Selfridges, £29.99

Aÿ is a wonderful Champagne village just outside Épernay and hugging the southern slopes of the Montagne de Reims. It's mostly famous because Bollinger is based there – and they're not in Aÿ by chance: they knew these slopes would produce fantastic base wine for their world-famous fizz. Smaller producers are now beginning to creep out of the shadows: this trend is one of the most encouraging features of the current Champagne scene. Giraud is one of these and offers us a truly classy glass. The bubbles foam and caress, the smell is of apples and spice, yet the flavour is quite serious behind the fizz – full and creamy, with gentle nut richness and savoury oatmeal, sharpened up with a streak of apple peel.

NV Champagne, Blanc de Blancs, Cuis 1er Cru, Pierre Gimonnet & Fils, France, 12.5% abv
Armit, £28.15

I've known Gimonnet for years – I think I've still got a bottle or two of 1990 vintage under the stairs – and this fascinating Chardonnay-based beauty reminds me why I used to buy it by the case. It's winsomely mild, gently creamy in texture, the bubbles foaming, caressing, not crackling on my tongue. That's the texture, but the flavour is much funkier – round and creamy, but the cream is more like Greek yoghurt or a very young goat's cheese mashed up with bruised pear skins. Lovely and slightly wild now, it'll be a punk star in two or three years.

2002 Champagne, Brut Special Reserve (P & C Heidsieck), France, 12% abv
Waitrose, £26.99

Wow, these 2002 Champagnes are beginning to rock and roll. This was always going to be an unusual vintage, with grapes literally being shrivelled on the vine by the sun and alcohol levels as high as they've been for 50 years. The question was not, are they any good? – they clearly were right from the second they were picked – but what kind of beautiful beast will they mature into? This Waitrose own-label 2002 is a good example. It's rich, it's classy, it's wild. Soft and fresh to start, with an apple blossom scent, such callow youthfulness is quickly brushed to one side by an almost leathery maturity, fruit like browned baked apple skins and a richness like bruised clotted cream and crème fraîche all piled on top of a Chelsea bun.

2005 Pelorus, Cloudy Bay, New Zealand, 12.5% abv
Majestic, £23.99 (but always on offer); Sainsbury's (selected stores), £17.99

This tastes like fine Champagne ought to taste, but rarely does – wonderfully fresh and bright, but fundamentally soft and ripe, its mellowness nipped by acidity, its fullness created not by sugar but by long contact with the creamy yeast lees that give this its fabulous hazelnut and oatmeal savoury character.

2002 Champagne, Les Pionniers (P & C Heidsieck), France, 12% abv Co-op, £20.99

It's encouraging to see our supermarkets making a real effort with their own-label Champagnes at a time when many of the big brands seem to be taking quality less seriously. This exhibits that lovely 2002 vintage ripeness, an almost chubby texture and flavour of strawberries and cream topped off with hazelnuts, but it's all in excellent balance and makes for a classy mouthful.

2004 Vintage Champagne (Union Champagne), France, 12.5% abv Tesco, £20.99

Tesco sell shed loads of Champagne, a good deal of it their utterly reliable, entirely enjoyable 1er Cru. They stick with the same supplier for their vintage – the Union Champagne co-operative at Avize, bang in the middle of the great Côte des Blancs Chardonnay vineyards. This 2004 is based on Chardonnay, mostly from Grand Cru vineyards (the best, superior even to Premier Cru). It's a very classy, classic style that you'd pay a lot more for if it was under a fancier label. Soft, mellow, creamy, nicely cut with acidity and the fruit of fresh apples, fattened up with hazelnut and the warm yeastiness of new-baked brioche.

2007 Cavendish, Ridgeview, East Sussex, England, 12% abv
Oddbins, £19.99, Jeroboams, £23.45

Ridgeview has become a very serious player in the sparkling wine world; it uses the classic Champagne grape varieties – Chardonnay, Pinot Noir and Pinot Meunier. There are several Ridgeview cuvées: the most widely available is probably Bloomsbury, but Cavendish is my current favourite. It has a full, loft apple fruit – a lot of good Champagnes traditionally have this slightly bruised flavour of apples stored in the loft for Christmas – and this is matched by some syrupy cream, a gentle nip from boiled lemon zest, and a final flavour of brioche crust. Pretty classic stuff.

2006 Cuvée John Inglis Hall, Breaky Bottom, East Sussex, England, 12% abv
Waitrose, £19.99

Peter Hall has been growing grapes in a hidden fold of the South Downs near Lewes for 36 years. He's now planted some Chardonnay, but Seyval Blanc – much derided in France – is what he's always believed in, and this fascinating Seyval sparkler is what made his reputation. Reserved, austere but full, mixing flavours of wood bark, dry apple pips and peel with porridgey cream and hazelnut, this almost stony-textured wine does reflect these chalky Sussex acres, does reflect the travails of an English vigneron's life, yet the calm patrician gentleness of the aftertaste reflects the mellow, wry contentment of the man himself.

NV Champagne, Brut Tradition, Marc Chauvet, France, 12% abv
Real Wine Co, £19.50

Rilly-la-Montagne is a strange little village on the Montagne de Reims, facing due north. There are several of these north-facing and, therefore, presumably colder and less sunny villages on the Montagne de Reims – and they all grow very good black grapes, which usually require more sun and heat than white grapes. Despite hundreds of years of discussion, no one has yet come up with a definitive explanation. All I can say is, the proof is in the bottle – in this case a fascinating wine from a long-established family of growers, based on black grapes, with a positively cedary scent that runs right through the wine, perfuming the apple peel, the cream and the honey bread as it goes.

NV Crémant de Bourgogne Brut Rosé, Blason de Bourgogne (Caves Bailly Lapierre), Burgundy, France, 12% abv
Waitrose, £12.99

Pink Champagne for less than half the money. Pink Champagne flavour, that is. This is made from Pinot Noir grapes grown just outside the Champagne region, but on the same soils. So the flavour is pretty much the same – dry, restrained, fresh apple fruit and a splash of Sicilian lemon acid and a slightly waxy, mellow pink feel rather than taste. Elegant, charming.

NV Deutz Marlborough Cuvée Brut, New Zealand, 12% abv Oddbins, £12.99

Deutz was one of the first Champagne houses to take the possibilities of the New World for top-class fizz seriously. In New Zealand Deutz is able to pick grapes full of tang and freshness and, using exactly the same methods and machinery as they'd use back in France, they turn out a fantastically good Champagne lookalike each year – full of apple fruit, cream and hazelnut softness and a bit of oatmeal savouriness left lingering in your mouth once the bubbles have fled.

NV Jansz Premium Rosé, Tasmania, Australia, 12.5% abv
Oddbins £12.99; Nidderdale Fine Wines, £13.50; Selfridges, £14.99

The UK seems to run out of this each year, and the reason might be quite simply that we can't get enough of it. I use it at tastings round the country whenever I can lay my hands on it, and people are clamouring at the end of the evening to know where they can buy it. So hurry. This very pale pink wine, with its delicate fresh strawberry flavour, its apple acid and its invigorating, foaming rush of bubbles won't be there if you dally.

NV Crémant de Loire, Pascal Pibaleau, Loire Valley, France, 12% abv
Christopher Piper Wines, £9.99

Fascinating, frothy, characterful, party pink. Pascal Pibaleau is based in Azay-le-Rideau, one of the first wine villages I ever visited; I poled up to a cave dug into the cliff on the banks of the Loire and said 'Could I taste your red?' 'We don't make red,' the bereted *paysan* replied, rather frostily. He probably made pink fizz. This is made from the local Grolleau and Cabernet Franc black grapes, and they impart a delightful flavour of pink apple flesh, peach and red plums all floating on a seductive sea of pale pink foam.

NV Prosecco, Il Fresco, Villa Sandi, Italy, 11% abv
Playford Ros, £9.34

Lovely, bright-eyed, gently foaming party fizz. It's the freshness, the lack of complexity, the gushing easy pleasy personality that makes Prosecco such a success. Prosecco offers us pear and apple flesh perfume, a twist of quite gentle lemon peel acidity and a softer foaming bubble than most other sparklers. What's not to like?
• Waitrose, M&S, Sainsbury's, Asda and Tesco all do good Prosecco.

NV Bellante, Brut Rosé (Bonotto), Veneto, Italy, 11%
Marks & Spencer, £8.99

This used to be called Prosecco Raboso. Italy recently changed its wine laws, and grapes like Raboso grown outside a specific Prosecco area can't use the Prosecco name any more. Never mind, the wine's the same – bright, blossoming, pale party pink, full of attractive pear flesh fruit and a touch of muscat, soft, scented, not quite dry, very easy-going to make your party swing.
• Waitrose has a similar wine called San Leo (£7.99) which also used to be labelled Prosecco.

NV Moscato Freisa Vino Spumante, Italy, 6.5% abv
Marks & Spencer, £7.99

Nothing serious here, just frothy fun. This is pale salmon pink and is a low-alcohol off-dry bubbly from white Moscato and red Freisa grapes. Floral perfume, grapy, soft fruit, a little icing sugar sweetness and a froth as fresh and iridescent as candy floss.

2007 Crémant du Jura, Chardonnay Brut, Philippe Michel, Jura, France, 12% abv Aldi, £6.99

The jewel in Aldi's crown. It has the soft ripe apple and mildly nutty cream of Chardonnay-based Champagne, but the Jura mountains have added an appetizing peppery bite and a lingering scent of orange blossom.

2008 Vintage Cava (Codorníu), Spain, 11.5% abv
Sainsbury's Taste the Difference, £6.99

Codorníu – Spain's best big fizz-maker – produces this for Sainsbury's, using 55% Chardonnay from its high-quality vineyards of Raimat near Lérida. It's got a good, persistent, foaming fizz, nice apple peel acidity and an intriguing orange-scented custard cream softness.

• Waitrose, M&S and the Co-op also do good own-label Cava.

2008 Lambrusco dell'Emilia, Camillo Donati, Italy, 12% abv
Les Caves de Pyrène, £12.99

I can't resist just squeezing this in. Real Lambrusco – utterly, utterly original. Mad, really. Dry, dense, fizzy. It smells of autumn leaves – slightly dank, but as soon as you finish your walk you'll have steak and kidney pud and crumpets. There's fruit – a cherry tart, or maybe cherries left at the bottom of a paper bag that have lost their crispness and started to brown. They're still cherries. Just. Hey, some orange peel, some rose water; it will take a leap of the imagination, but this is just crying out for a 'real' Bolognese, or a strip of glistening hot fat off a freshly grilled bistecca.

FORTIFIED WINES

One of the signs that consumer interest in fortified wines is waning must be the consolidation of supply on the High Street. A very few producers dominate the supermarkets' supply of fortified wines – less than the fingers on one hand for the good ones. The good sherry guys are basically divided between Lustau and Williams & Humbert, and the good port guys are in effect divided between the Symington Family – they make ports like Graham's, Dow's and Warre's – and the Fladgate Partnership who make Taylor's, Fonseca and Croft; they often use the name Quinta & Vineyard Bottlers on own-label ports. The first thing I should say is – thank goodness such a quality-conscious bunch do dominate our High Streets. But homogeneity is the price we pay, particularly in our dry sherries and our mid-range ports, which are generally pretty good and generally pretty similar to each other. Diversity either comes at a higher price or in the less frenetic byways of our wine world – Tanners of Shrewsbury and The Wine Society would be good places to start.

- In this section you will find sherries first, then ports, in descending price order.

SHERRY

The Society's Exhibition Viejo Oloroso Dulce Sherry (Sanchez Romate), Spain, 20% abv
Wine Society, £10.95

Good, rich, brown sherry. The sweeter styles have been given a bad name by companies simply adding sweet brown goo to dry sherry, shaking it up and calling it 'cream' or 'sweet' or whatever. A rich, sweet sherry must have a structure, a weight, some gravitas to stop it from being sugar water – and this can only come from long aging in barrels and careful blending, cask by cask. Here, the richness of raisins and dates and syrup of figs is refreshingly seasoned by an almost cedary scent from the old barrels where the wine spent long years undisturbed, gradually forming its character with the slow passage of time.

Manzanilla, La Gitana, Hidalgo, Spain, 15% abv
Widely available, £8.39

Good dry sherries have nothing to hide behind, no make-up, no fancy dress. They hint at a richness they don't really have, and they try to camouflage the gauntness which they actually possess. You can't really find ways to make them fit into the dry white mainstream (Chardonnay, Sauvignon and Pinot Grigio) without destroying all that they stand for. Of all my favourites, La Gitana probably makes the best stab at crossing the divide. It is uncompromisingly dry, yet displays a mellowness of bread crust and hazelnut that soothes the dry, dusty, old-wood austerity, and all the flavours merge into a creamy texture that hints at richness yet stays bright and mouthwatering – and bone dry.

Fino del Puerto Sherry, Solera Jerezana, Spain, 16.5% abv
Waitrose, £8.19

An excellent example of dry sherry: assertive, woody, redolent of the dark cellars full of fumes from barrels of maturing wines, where sherry sleeps for year on year before offering itself to market. You can taste the dry wood in this wine, but it's very dry, not a bit vanilla-ish like the wood flavour of some oaky New World whites. This has an incisive, cutting edge and a scent of old floorboards or banisters that worms its way inside your palate in an attractively insidious way. It does hint at a soft belly of almonds and brioche crust, but it's never more than a suggestion.

Dry Amontillado Sherry, Aged 12 years, Emilio Lustau, Spain, 19% abv
Sainsbury's Taste the Difference, £6.29/50 cl

Dry Amontillado is a rare but wonderful drink with a very particular flavour of buttered brazils – brazil nuts coated with a buttery caramel. This example hints at buttered brazils, but doesn't give you them full on. That's its minus point. Its plus point is that this is very good, full, amber-brown, rich yet dry sherry. It's austere and challenging, because despite being full of the flavours of dates and raisins and nutty syrup, it's as though all their sweetness has been sucked out of them by a vacuum pump, leaving a very dry, haughty, yet satisfyingly rich, dark wine.

Dry Oloroso Sherry, Aged 12 Years, Emilio Lustau, Spain, 20% abv
Sainsbury's Taste the Difference, £6.29/50 cl

Relatively soft but pretty dry and quite dense. Oloroso often has a bit more bite than this, but the gentle, warm syrup of nuts and figs, and the essence of raisins and dates – these are the flavours I want, even if this is a rather mild expression of the style.

Manzanilla Sherry (Williams & Humbert), Spain, 15% abv
Marks & Spencer, £5.99

This is quite a bargain, because it's classy wine made by a top producer for M&S. Very fresh, very dry, as dry as beach pebbles in the sun, and bright and crackly as twigs in high summer. The fruit, if it's there, is like the core of a bone dry apple sucked of its sweetness, and the scent is of ancient dusty wood that has seen many, many silent years drift by.

MADEIRA

Full Rich Madeira, Henriques & Henriques, Portugal, 19% abv
Waitrose, £11.49; also at Bennetts Fine Wines, Fortnum & Mason and others

Henriques & Henriques makes a very good range of well-matured Madeiras from single grape varieties, ranging from startlingly dry to rich and deep. But I suspect most of you never drink Madeira, so I thought I'd suggest this as an introduction to its unique, smoky, acid yet sweet flavours. This is made from an all-purpose grape called Tinta Negra Mole – a lot of basic Madeira uses this grape. This example is rich and sweet with a flavour of baked old brown fruit made exciting by acidity and an island saltiness. That baked flavour is achieved by heating the wine in vats to about 50°C for three months – cooking it, in effect. In the old days, they sent the wine on ships across the Equator to bake. If you've never tried Madeira, here's where to start.

PORT

1996 Vintage Port, Fonseca Guimaraens, Portugal, 20.5% abv
Bibendum, Sainsbury's, Waitrose, c.£24.99

This Fonseca is a triumph for the traditional, for the great old drink that port used to be when with every mouthful you revelled in its richness and sensual scent and you also could sense the alarm bells jangling in its depths warning you to take care. Fonseca is a superb port maker, probably the keenest of any of the big boys to preserve perfume and a sense of individuality in its wines. It does so triumphantly here; the wine has a waxy, glyceriny weight perfectly balanced by acidity mixed with a palate-nipping hint of bitterness and a definite glimpse of pepper and herbs. But all this provides a daybed for the glorious blackberry and blackcurrant fruit, the whisper of floral scent and the warm glow of exotic spice.

1990 Colheita, Tawny Porto, Cálem, Portugal, 20% abv
Wine Society, £21

A fascinating glimpse of the old world of port, when time wasn't money and a wine was sold only when it was ready to sell – even if it took 20 years' aging to get it to the perfect point. Colheita wines are from a single harvest but aged in barrel, not bottle. Vintage port is aged in bottle, and is dark and purple. Tawny ports are the amber ones which are aged in barrel, but these are almost always blended together and sold without a vintage date on the label. Colheita tawny port – single vintage tawny port – is a great rarity. It has a lovely tawny colour just tinged with a russet blush, and the fruit is old and smooth – almonds and raisins, dates and figs – yet not so smooth that there isn't a flicker of lime zest acidity and the nuzzling bitterness of pistachio skins. There's even a savoury edge to its nut and raisin syrup sweetness.

2000 Late Bottled Vintage Port, Warre's, Portugal, 20% abv
Waitrose, £19.99

Four years softening in cask followed by six years maturing in the bottle means that this is vastly superior to the commercial LBV ports on the market. Age has mellowed its texture, which now has no hard edges but impressive power and warmth; its blackberry fruit has become almost syrupy, with a spice and raisin richness that is still fresh and appetizing.

1994 Vintage Port (Symington Family Estates), Portugal, 20% abv
Tesco Finest, £16.49

This is a bargain. How can it be, at 16 quid? Well, it's 16 years old. That's a pound a year – because you can't enjoy this kind of quality if the wine's only a few years old. To get this marvellous mellow richness, the wine needs age. The producers have aged it for us – and they're charging a quid a year. Think about it! Then buy a bottle and see what I'm on about. Dark, rich, yet scented, lustrous, lush blackberry and loganberry fruit, powerful and slightly bitter at the edge – you need that bitterness to combat the hedonistic rush of fruit syrup trailed with woodsmoke and simply bursting with the warmth and sunshine of the fabulous 1994 vintage.

Crusted Port (bottled in 2002), Graham's, Portugal, 20% abv
Sainsbury's, £16.46

Crusted port is a sort of 'halfway to vintage' style. It's not as intense and thunderous as vintage port, but has much of the gorgeous scented fruit of a true vintage wine. This one is all about blackberries and superripe loganberries hemmed in by fairly muscular tannin and peppery aggression, but with a lovely orchard autumn scent as well.

Terra Prima Reserve Port, Fonseca, Portugal, 20% abv
Bibendum, Waitrose, £15.99

Fonseca makes majestic traditional ports but it also has its finger firmly on the pulse of innovation. This is very modern stuff – fantastically and immediately attractive, almost irresistible in its heady scent and lush, smooth fruit – yet is clearly a wine of enormous quality born of generations of experience. It's captured the floral scent of violets and rose petals and swathed it in a richness of sweet cherries and juicy plums with vanilla coconut, suggesting that it's been aged for a few months in new oak barrels.

Pink Port, Croft, Portugal, 19.5% abv
Co-op, Morrisons, Sainsbury's, Tesco, Virgin, £10–11

These pink ports. I'm sure they're the cause of much apoplexy in the dining rooms of London West End clubs – well, that's if the inmates have noticed them; unlikely I suppose – but I think they're great. I love this whoosh of day-glo pink, electric, metallic pink, punk pink for a wine that's hardly out of nappies but just burbles and chortles with party fruit – raspberry, pears and cherry blossom too.
- M&S own-label Pink Port (£7.99) is also good.

Ruby Port, Portugal, 20% abv Sainsbury's, £7.86

There are several gutsy basic ports on the market. This is my favourite this year – not at all subtle but rich and dense and full of chewy, stewy dark fruit – it hits the spot on a cold, wet winter night.
- Asda's Ruby Port (£5.87) is also pretty good.

SWEETIES

Sweet wine is such a fashion victim. There was a time when you couldn't turn up for supper without someone wheeling out a bottle of Muscat de Beaumes-de-Venise, probably a supermarket own-label. Remember that? It's still made, and it's still very good, it's just that we've moved on, and our supermarkets have said, fine, we try to offer our customers what they want. If they don't want such sweet delights any more, we won't stock them. In bean counters' terms, you can see their point, although with supermarkets increasingly dominant in our British wine market, you'd hope they would see some advantage in trying to lead us back to sweet wine. But I suppose in tough times like today, if we have to cut something from our drinks basket, sweet wine, which almost always needs to be expensive to be any good, is a bit of a no-brainer. Ah well, at least it means this is an area where our independent merchants can set out to hand-sell these objects of delight and desire. Let's hope they take up the challenge. Sweet Muscats have been included in this section rather than the fortified section because they're pudding wines at heart.

- The wines are listed in descending price order.
- Many sweet wines are sold in half bottles (375ml) or 500ml bottles.

2002 Voudomato, Hatzidakis, Santorini, Greece, 11% abv
Les Caves de Pyrène, £24.99/375ml

The Greek island of Santorini has just about the wildest vineyards you'll find anywhere in Europe, so I suppose I shouldn't be surprised to come across a rip-roaring, mind-expanding novelty like this. The grape variety is called 'L'oeil de boeuf', or ox-eye. I don't know what ox-eye tastes like when it's fresh and young, but this is wild, rasping, sweet-sour, age-old, saturated black fruits fading to brown, their freshness gone, but their sweetness hanging in there. Cherry skins, stewed cranberries, a breeze carrying hillside herbs to ruffle the torpid aroma of vestries and prayer books.

2006 Málaga, Selección Especial, Jorge Ordóñez, Spain, 13% abv
Oddbins, £16.49/500ml

Málaga wine, to most people, means the sticky brown stuff you buy at the airport on the way home and then spend the next 12 months wondering why, and who on earth can you offload it on. But there's another Málaga, harking back to the days when Málaga was a great and revered wine region. It's hardly made nowadays, but the Muscat grapes that cling to the hills above the town give a wine that is bright and crunchy, sweet yet fresh, full of greengage, grapefruit and ripe green muscatel fruit, rubbed with stones and sap, scented with mint leaf and basil.

2008 Riesling, Sweet Agnes, Seifried Estate, Nelson, New Zealand, 10% abv
Laithwaites, £14.99/375ml

The Seifried family are a hardy bunch from solid Austrian winemaking stock, and used to the European philosophy that you need to make the vines suffer to bring out the best in their fruit. So hats off to Hermann Seifried for making what is a real rarity – New Zealand ice wine made from frozen grapes. The thing about frozen grapes is that it's the water that turns into ice, not the sugar. The sugar merely intensifies, so if you press the grapes at below zero – not difficult in Central Europe, not so easy in New Zealand – the syrup separates from the ice, and you get fantastically sweet juice to make into wine. And this is a good example: laden with peach and pineapple syrup sweetness, but, in the classic ice wine way, streaked through with powerful lime juice acidity, and flecked with herbs and smoke.

2008 Viognier-Pinot Gris-Marsanne, The Noble Mud Pie, d'Arenberg, Adelaide, South Australia, 8.5% abv
Oddbins, £14.49/375ml

Does d'Arenberg actually want to sell this wine or not? Have a glass of Noble Mud Pie. Don't mind if I don't. D'Arenberg never labels its wines with names that are remotely relevant to what's inside the bottle (Dead Arm Shiraz is one of its top wines). But it works. D'Arenberg is a big success in the British market, and originality in labels and flavour are the reason why. I haven't come across anyone mixing these three grapes together before – but it sure works, and it sure is wild. Baked Bramley apples swirled with quince jelly and fresh orange juice, scented with honeysuckle and mango nectar, made wise and golden with barley sugar. Sultry, dripping with the heavy-lidded gold of an autumn orchard.

2006 Gaillac Doux, Renaissance, Domaine Rotier, South-West France, 14% abv
Big Red Wine Company, £13.95/500ml

Gaillac, in South-West France, has a great history of sweet winemaking, but, until very recently, an extremely drab present based on dry whites and chewy rough reds. So to see sweet wines being revived is a thrill, because it's far more difficult to make fine sweet

wine than dry wine. Made from the wonderfully-named Loin de l'oeil grape, and fermented and aged in oak barrels, this wine is rich and fat, not hysterically sweet, but waxy and dripping with quince, fresh figs and honey, with a funky mix of melon, pineapple chunks and marrow jam unexpectedly appearing on your tongue just before the wine drifts off into a delightful aftertaste of strawberry and honey.

2006 Sauternes, Château Suduiraut/Waitrose, Bordeaux, France, 14.5% abv
Waitrose, £13.49/375ml

Château Suduiraut is one of the smartest properties in Sauternes, but it isn't easy to sell Sauternes nowadays and so when an outfit like Waitrose comes along and says, 'What about an own label?', well, you might want to pull yourself up to a great height and shout 'Who do you think you're talking to?', but in fact you give in gracefully and direct the buyers to some very decent barrels that haven't quite merited being bottled under the Château's own label. So this isn't cheap, but you'd be paying a lot more if it didn't have the Waitrose name on the label. This is classic Sauternes, not intensely sweet, but succulent in a honeyed, waxy way, glyceriny in its weight, peach and pineapple fruit evident but not excessive and a whiff of savoury scent or woodsmoke from the wine's aging in oak barrels.

• Tesco has a pretty good own-label 2005 Sauternes (£12.29 for a 375ml bottle).

2009 Noble Sauvignon Blanc, The Ned, Marlborough, New Zealand, 12% abv
Majestic, £12.99/375ml

The Ned is a new label from Brent Marris, the guy originally behind the wildly successful Wither Hills brand. The Ned majors in Sauvignon Blanc dry wines, but there's a growing interest in sweet wines in New

Zealand. Most of them employ Riesling fruit – yet since Sauvignon is a crucial component in Bordeaux's Sauternes, it's a pretty small step to leaving a corner of your Sauvignon vineyard to overripen way after the normal harvest, and see what you can come up with. Well, this is pretty good. It's honey-rich, but never loses sight of the refreshing green leaf acidity of Marlborough Sauvignon Blanc.

Museum Muscat, Yalumba, Victoria, Australia, 18% abv
Flagship Wines, Nidderdale Fine Wines, Noel Young Wines, c.£12.50/375ml; Virgin Wines, £11.49

These marvellous sweet brown wines are drenched in the history of Australia. The grapes are grown in the old gold fields of north-east Victoria. After 150 years the gold mines are being revived, but the vines never left, and the style of wine has never changed. Each year the tiny crop of sun-blistered grapes is gathered, the syrupy juice squeezed from the shrivelled skins, then fermentation begins – just momentarily, sometimes for hardly a day. Then high-strength alcohol is added to the super-sweet juice: the yeasts are killed, fermentation stops, and you're left with the sheer essence of the Muscat grape. Over time, this wine will be blended and blended and blended again – we're talking decades here, generations, and sometimes even longer, because this Museum Muscat will include a tiny amount of wine that was made 100 years ago. Rose petal perfume, mixed with the intensity of muscovado moist brown sugar, nectar dripping from ripe figs as the wasps gather, a syrup of honey and dates and a refreshing streak of bitter-sweet marmalade orange peel.

2003 Moscatel de Setúbal, Colheita, Bacalhôa, Portugal, 17.5% abv
Tanners, £8.20

This seems like wine from another age, and I suppose it is, because Moscatel de Setúbal, made just south of Lisbon, is one of Portugal's more ancient styles, clinging to life in our high-tension modern world through the support of companies like Tanners of Shrewsbury. This is certainly sweet, but not unctuously so, because the ancient brown juices of fig and prune are mingled with a rich orange syrup of peel and marmalade, scented with cumin and sage and roughened by the bitter beauty of freshly milled spice.

2005 Monbazillac, Château Vari, Monbazillac, South-West France, 13% abv
Christopher Piper Wines, £6.99/375ml

Monbazillac is the sweet wine of Bergerac, Bordeaux's neighbour to the south-east. It's made from the same grapes as Bordeaux's famous Sauternes – a blend of Sémillon and Sauvignon Blanc – and used to be thought of as Sauternes-lite. But recently growers have been making wine that certainly equals Sauternes in quality and style. This is more of an aperitif-style, but it has the signature waxy texture, good quince and pear syrup sweetness and an attractive savoury fatness a bit like cream cheese.

2006 Late Harvest Sauvignon Blanc, Reserva Privada, Concha y Toro, Maule, Chile, 12% abv
Booths, Majestic, Oddbins, Tesco, Flagship Wines and other independents, £5.99/375ml

One of the real bargains of the sweet wine world. Chile doesn't have much track record for sweet wines, but the Sauvignon Blanc grape is an integral part of Sauternes – the famous French sweet wine – and this late-harvest version manages to be rich and fairly honey-sweet without ever losing the tangy, leafy Sauvignon Blanc acidity.

Storing, serving and tasting

Wine is all about enjoyment, so don't let anyone make you anxious about opening, serving, tasting and storing it. Here are some tips to help you enjoy your wine all the more.

The corkscrew

The first step in tasting any wine is to extract the cork. Look for a corkscrew with an open spiral and a comfortable handle. The Screwpull brand is far and away the best, with a high-quality open spiral. 'Waiter's friend' corkscrews – the type you see used in restaurants – are good too, once you get the knack.

Corkscrews with a solid core that looks like a giant woodscrew tend to mash up delicate corks or get stuck in tough ones. And try to avoid those 'butterfly' corkscrews with the twin lever arms and a bottle opener on the end; they tend to leave cork crumbs floating in the wine.

Corks

Don't be a cork snob. The only requirements for the seal on a bottle of wine are that it should be hygienic, airtight, long-lasting and removable. Real cork is environmentally friendly, but is prone to shrinkage and infection, which can taint the wine. Synthetic closures modelled on the traditional cork are common in budget wines, but the largest increase has been in the use of screwcaps, or Stelvin closures, which are now appearing on some very classy wines, especially in Australia and New Zealand, South Africa and South America.

Decanting

Transferring wine to a decanter brings it into contact with oxygen, which can open up the flavours. You don't need to do this ages before serving and you don't need a special decanter: a glass jug is just as good. And there's no reason why you shouldn't decant the wine to aerate it, then pour it back into its bottle to serve it.

Mature red wine is likely to contain sediment and needs careful handling. Stand the bottle upright for a day or two to let the sediment fall to the bottom. Open the wine carefully, and place a torch or candle beside the decanter. As you pour, stand so that you can see the light shining through the neck of the bottle. Pour the wine into the decanter in one steady motion and stop when you see the sediment reaching the neck of the bottle.

Temperature

The temperature of wine has a bearing on its flavour. Heavy reds are happy at room temperature, but the lighter the wine the cooler it should be. I'd serve Burgundy and other Pinot Noir reds at cool larder temperature. Juicy, fruity young reds, such as wines from the Loire Valley, are refreshing served lightly chilled.

Chilling white wines makes them taste fresher, but also subdues flavours, so bear this in mind if you're splashing out on a top-quality white – don't keep it in the fridge too long. Sparkling wines, however, must be well chilled to avoid exploding corks and fountains of foam.

For quick chilling, fill a bucket with ice and cold water, plus a few spoonfuls of salt if you're in a real hurry. This is much more effective than ice on its own. If the wine is already cool, a vacuum-walled cooler will maintain the temperature.

The wine glass

The ideal wine glass is a fairly large tulip shape, made of fine, clear glass, with a slender stem. This shape helps to concentrate the aromas of the wine and to show off its colours and texture. For sparkling wine choose a tall, slender glass, as it helps the bubbles to last longer.

Look after your glasses carefully. Detergent residues or grease can affect the flavour of any wine and reduce the bubbliness of sparkling wine. Ideally, wash glasses in very hot water and don't use detergent at all. Rinse glasses thoroughly and allow them to air-dry. Store wine glasses upright to avoid trapping stale odours.

Keeping opened bottles

Exposure to oxygen causes wine to deteriorate. Once opened, it will last fairly well for a couple of days if you just push the cork back in and stick the bottle in the fridge, but you can also buy a range of effective devices to help keep oxygen at bay. Vacuvin uses a rubber stopper and a vacuum pump to remove air from the bottle. Others inject inert gas into the bottle to shield the wine from the ravages of oxidation.

Laying down wine

The longer you intend to keep wine before you drink it, the more important it is to store it with care. If you haven't got a cellar, find a nook – under the stairs, a built-in cupboard or a disused fireplace – that is cool, relatively dark and vibration-free, in which you can store the bottles on their sides to keep the corks moist (if a cork dries out it will let air in and spoil the wine).

Wine should be kept cool – around 10–15°C/50–55°F. It is also important to avoid sudden temperature changes or extremes: a windowless garage or outhouse may be cool in summer but may freeze in winter. Exposure to light can ruin wine, but dark bottles go some way to protecting it from light.

How to taste wine

If you just knock your wine back like a cold beer, you'll be missing most of whatever flavour it has to offer. Take a bit of time to pay attention to what you're tasting and I guarantee you'll enjoy the wine more.

Read the label

There's no law that says you have to make life hard for yourself when tasting wine. So have a look at what you're drinking and read the notes on the back label if there is one. The label will tell you the vintage, the region and/or the grape variety, the producer and the alcohol level.

Look at the wine

Pour the wine into a glass so it is a third full and tilt it against a white background so you can enjoy the range of colours in the wine. Is it dark or light? Is it viscous or watery? As you gain experience, the look of the wine will tell you one or two things about the age and the likely flavour and weight of the wine. As a wine ages, whites lose their springtime greenness and gather deeper, golden hues, whereas red wines trade the purple of youth for a paler brick red.

Swirl and sniff

Give the glass a vigorous swirl to wake up the aromas in the wine, stick your nose in and inhale gently. This is where you'll be hit by the amazing range of smells a wine can produce. Interpret them in any way that means something to you personally: it's only by reacting honestly to the taste and smell of a wine that you can build up a memory bank of flavours against which to judge future wines.

Take a sip

At last! It's time to drink the wine. So take a decent-sized slurp – enough to fill your mouth about a third full. The tongue can detect only very basic flavour elements: sweetness at the tip, acidity at the sides and bitterness at the back. The real business of tasting goes on in a cavity at the back of the mouth that is really part of the nose. The idea is to get the fumes from the wine to rise up into this nasal cavity. Note the toughness, acidity and sweetness of the wine, then suck some air through the wine to help the flavours on their way. Gently 'chew' the wine and let it coat your tongue, teeth, cheeks and gums. Jot down a few notes as you form your opinion and then make the final decision… Do you like it or don't you?

Swallow or spit it out

If you are tasting a lot of wines, you will have to spit as you go if you want to remain upright and retain your judgement. Otherwise, go ahead and swallow and enjoy the lovely aftertaste of the wine.

Wine faults

If you order wine in a restaurant and you find one of these faults you are entitled to a replacement. Many retailers will also replace a faulty bottle if you return it the day after you open it, with your receipt. Sometimes faults affect random bottles, others may ruin a whole case of wine.

- Cork taint – a horrible musty, mouldy smell indicates 'corked' wine, caused by a contaminated cork.
- Volatile acidity – pronounced vinegary or acetone smells.
- Oxidation – sherry-like smells are not appropriate in red and white wines.
- Hydrogen sulphide – 'rotten eggs' smell.

Watchpoints

- Sediment in red wines makes for a gritty, woody mouthful. To avoid this, either decant the wine or simply pour it gently, leaving the last few centilitres of wine in the bottle.
- White crystals, or tartrates, on the cork or at the bottom of bottles of white wine are both harmless and flavourless.
- Sticky bottle neck – if wine has seeped past the cork it probably hasn't been very well kept and air might have got in. This may mean oxidized wine.
- Excess sulphur dioxide is sometimes noticeable as a smell of a recently struck match; it should dissipate after a few minutes.

Wine style guide

When faced with a shelf – or a screen – packed with wines from around the world, where do you start? Well, if you're after a particular flavour, my guide to wine styles will point you in the right direction.

White wines

Bone-dry, neutral whites

Neutral wines exist for the sake of seafood or to avoid interrupting you while you're eating. It's a question of balance, rather than aromas and flavours, but there will be a bit of lemon, yeast and a mineral thrill in a good Muscadet *sur lie* or a proper Chablis. Loads of Italian whites do the same thing, but Italy is increasingly picking up on the global shift towards fruit flavours and maybe some oak. Basic, cheap South African whites are often a good bet if you want something thirst-quenching and easy to drink. Colombard and Chenin are fairly neutral grape varieties widely used in South Africa, often producing appley flavours, and better examples add a lick of honey.

- Muscadet
- Chenin Blanc and Colombard – from the Loire Valley, South-West France, Australia, California or South Africa
- Basic white Bordeaux and Entre-Deux-Mers
- Chablis
- Pinot Grigio

Green, tangy whites

For nerve-tingling refreshment, Sauvignon Blanc is the classic grape, full of fresh grass, gooseberry and nettle flavours. I always used to go for New Zealand versions, but I'm now more inclined to reach for an inexpensive bottle from Chile, South Africa or Hungary. Or even a simple white Bordeaux, because suddenly

Bordeaux Sauvignon is buzzing with life. Most Sancerre and the other Loire Sauvignons are overpriced. Austria's Grüner Veltliner has a peppery freshness. From north-west Iberia, Galicia's Albariño grape has a stony, mineral lemon zest sharpness; the same grape is used in Portugal, for Vinho Verde. Alternatively, look at Riesling: Australia serves it up with aggressive lime and mineral flavours, and New Zealand and Chile give milder versions of the same style. Alsace Riesling is lemony and dry, while German Rieslings go from bone-dry to intensely sweet, with the tangiest, zestiest, coming from the Mosel Valley.

• Sauvignon Blanc – from New Zealand, Chile, Hungary, South Africa, or Bordeaux
• Loire Valley Sauvignons such as Sancerre and Pouilly-Fumé
• Riesling – from Australia, Austria, Chile, Germany, New Zealand, or Alsace in France
• Austrian Grüner Veltliner
• Vinho Verde from Portugal and Albariño from north-west Spain

Intense, nutty whites

The best white Burgundy from the Côte d'Or cannot be bettered for its combination of soft nut and oatmeal flavours, subtle, buttery oak and firm, dry structure. Prices are often hair-raising and the cheaper wines rarely offer much Burgundy style. For around £8–10 your best bet is oaked Chardonnay from an innovative Spanish region such as Somontano, or around Limoux in South-West France. You'll get a nutty, creamy taste and nectarine fruit with good oak-aged white Bordeaux or traditional white Rioja. Top Chardonnays from New World countries – and Italy for that matter – can emulate Burgundy, but we're looking at serious prices.

• White Burgundy – including Meursault, Pouilly-Fuissé, Chassagne-Montrachet, Puligny-Montrachet
• White Bordeaux – including Pessac-Léognan, Graves
• White Rioja
• Chardonnay from New Zealand and Oregon – and top examples from Australia, California and South Africa

Ripe, toasty whites

Aussie Chardonnay conquered the world with its upfront flavours of peaches, apricots and melons, usually spiced up by the vanilla, toast and butterscotch richness of new oak. This winning style has now become a standard-issue flavour produced by all sorts of countries, though I still love the original. You'll need to spend a bit more than a fiver nowadays if you want something to relish beyond the first glass. Oaked Australian Semillon can also give rich, ripe fruit flavours, as can oaked Chenin Blanc from South Africa. If you see the words 'unoaked' or 'cool-climate' on an Aussie bottle, expect an altogether leaner drink.

- Chardonnay: from Australia, Chile, California, South Africa
- Oak-aged Chenin Blanc from South Africa
- Australian Semillon

Aromatic whites

Alsace has always been a plentiful source of perfumed, dry or off-dry whites: Gewurztraminer with its rose and lychee scent or Muscat with its floral, hothouse grape perfume. A few producers in New Zealand, Australia, Chile and South Africa are having some success with these grapes. Floral, apricotty Viognier, traditionally the grape of Condrieu in the northern Rhône, now appears in vins de pays from all over southern France and also from California and Australia. Condrieu is expensive (£20 will get you entry-level stuff and no guarantee that it will be fragrant); vin de pays wines start at around £5 and are just as patchy. For aroma on a budget, grab some Hungarian Irsai Olivér or Argentinian Torrontés. English white wines often have a fresh, floral hedgerow scent – the Bacchus grape is one of the leaders of this style.

- Alsace whites, especially Gewurztraminer and Muscat
- Gewürztraminer from Austria, Chile, Germany, New Zealand and cooler regions of Australia
- Condrieu, from the Rhône Valley in France
- Viognier from southern France, Argentina, Australia, California, Chile
- English white wines, especially Bacchus
- Irsai Olivér and Cserszegi Füszeres from Hungary
- Torrontés from Argentina

Golden, sweet whites

Good sweet wines are difficult to make and therefore expensive: prices for Sauternes and Barsac (from Bordeaux) can go through the roof, but near-neighbours Monbazillac, Loupiac, Saussignac and Ste-Croix-du-Mont are more affordable. Sweet Loire wines such as Quarts de Chaume, Bonnezeaux and some Vouvrays have a quince aroma and a fresh acidity that can keep them lively for decades, as do sweet Rieslings such as Alsace Vendange Tardive, German and Austrian Beerenauslese (BA), Trockenbeeren-auslese (TBA) and Eiswein. Canadian icewine is quite rare over here, but we're seeing more of Hungary's Tokaji, with its sweet-sour, marmalade flavours.

- Sauternes, Barsac, Loupiac, Sainte-Croix-du-Mont
- Monbazillac, Saussignac, Jurançon and Pacherenc du Vic-Bilh from South-West France
- Loire sweet whites such as Bonnezeaux, Quarts de Chaume and Vouvray moelleux
- Auslese, Beerenauslese and Trockenbeerenauslese from Germany and Austria
- Eiswein from Germany, icewine from Canada
- Botrytis Semillon, Riesling or Gewürztraminer from Australia

Red wines

Juicy, fruity reds

The definitive modern style for easy-going reds. Tasty, refreshing and delicious with or without food, they pack in loads of crunchy fruit while minimizing the tough, gum-drying tannins that characterize most traditional red wine styles. Beaujolais (made from the Gamay grape) is the prototype – and if you're distinctly underwhelmed by the very mention of the word 'Beaujolais', remember that the delightfully named Fleurie, St-Amour and Chiroubles also come from the Beaujolais region. Loire reds such as Chinon and Saumur (made from Cabernet Franc) pack in the fresh raspberries. Italy's Bardolino is light and refreshing, as is young Valpolicella. Nowadays, hi-tech producers all over the world are working the magic with a whole host of grape varieties. Carmenère, Malbec and Merlot are always good bets, and Grenache/Garnacha and Tempranillo usually come up with the goods. Italian grapes like Bonarda, Barbera and Sangiovese seem to double in succulence under Argentina's blazing sun. And at around £6–7 even Cabernet Sauvignon – if it's from somewhere warm like Australia, South America, South Africa or Spain – or a vin de pays Syrah from southern France, will emphasize the fruit and hold back on the tannin.

- Beaujolais – including Brouilly, Chiroubles, Fleurie, Juliénas, Moulin-à-Vent, St-Amour. Also wines made from the Gamay grape in other parts of France
- Loire reds: Chinon, Saumur, Saumur-Champigny – and, if you're lucky, Bourgueil, Cheverny and St-Nicolas-de-Bourgueil
- Grenache (from France) and Garnacha (from Spain)
- Carmenère from Chile
- Basic Merlot from just about anywhere
- Inexpensive Argentinian reds, especially Bonarda, but also Sangiovese and Tempranillo

Silky, strawberryish reds

Here we're looking for some special qualities, specifically a gorgeously smooth texture and a heavenly fragrance of strawberries, raspberries or cherries. We're looking for soft, decadent, seductive wines.

One grape – Pinot Noir – and one region – Burgundy – stand out, but prices are high to astronomical. Good red Burgundy is addictively hedonistic and all sorts of strange decaying aromas start to hover around the strawberries as the wine ages. Pinot Noirs from New Zealand, California, Oregon and, increasingly, Australia come close, but they're expensive, too; Chilean Pinots are far more affordable. You can get that strawberry perfume (though not the silky texture) from other grapes in Spain's Navarra, Rioja and up-coming regions like La Mancha and Murcia. Southern Rhône blends can deliver if you look for fairly light examples of Côtes du Rhône-Villages or Costières de Nîmes.

- Red Burgundy – including Chassagne-Montrachet, Beaune, Givry, Nuits-St-Georges, Pommard
- Pinot Noir from Australia, California, Chile, New Zealand, Oregon
- Spanish reds from Rioja, Navarra, La Mancha and Valdepeñas, especially with Tempranillo as the main grape
- Red blends from the southern Rhône Valley, such as Costières de Nîmes, Côtes du Rhône-Villages, Gigondas
- Australian Grenache

Intense, blackcurrant reds

Firm, intense wines which often only reveal their softer side with a bit of age; Cabernet Sauvignon is the grape, on its own or blended with Merlot or other varieties. Bordeaux is the classic region but there are far too many overpriced underachievers there. And Cabernet's image has changed. You can still choose the austere, tannic style, in theory aging to a heavenly cassis and cedar maturity, but most of the world is taking a fruitier blackcurrant-and-mint approach. Chile does the fruity style par excellence. New Zealand can deliver Bordeaux-like flavours, but in a faster-maturing wine. Australia often adds a medicinal eucalyptus twist or a dollop of blackcurrant jam. Argentina and South Africa are making their mark too. In Spain, Ribera del Duero can also come up with blackcurrant flavours.

- Bordeaux reds such as Côtes de Castillon, St-Émilion, Pomerol
- Cabernet Sauvignon from just about anywhere
- Cabernet Sauvignon-Merlot blends

Spicy, warm-hearted reds

Australian Shiraz is the epitome of this rumbustious, riproaring style: dense, rich, chocolaty, sometimes with a twist of pepper, a whiff of smoke, or a slap of leather. But it's not alone. There are southern Italy's Primitivo and Nero d'Avola, California's Zinfandel, Mexico's Petite Sirah, Argentina's Malbec, South Africa's Pinotage, Toro from Spain and some magnificent Greek reds. In southern France the wines of the Languedoc often show this kind of warmth, roughed up with hillside herbs. And if you want your spice more serious, more smoky and minerally, go for the classic wines of the northern Rhône Valley.

- Australian Shiraz, as well as blends of Shiraz with Grenache and Mourvèdre/Mataro – and Durif
- Northern Rhône Syrah (Cornas, Côte-Rôtie, Hermitage, St-Joseph) and southern Rhône blends such as Châteauneuf-du-Pape
- Southern French reds, such as Corbières, Coteaux du Languedoc, Côtes du Roussillon, Faugères, Fitou, Minervois
- Italian reds such as Primitivo, Aglianico, Negroamaro and Nero d'Avola
- Zinfandel and Petite Sirah reds
- Argentinian Malbec
- South African Pinotage

Mouthwatering, sweet-sour reds

Sounds weird? This style is primarily the preserve of Italy, and it's all about food: the rasp of sourness cuts through rich, meaty food, with a lip-smacking tingle that works equally well with pizza or tomato-based pasta dishes. But there's fruit in there too – cherries and plums – plus raisiny sweetness and a herby bite. The wines are now better made than ever, with more seductive fruit, but holding on to those fascinating flavours. All sorts of native Italian grape varieties deliver this delicious sour-cherries taste: Sangiovese (the classic red grape of Tuscany), Nebbiolo (from Piedmont), Barbera, Dolcetto, Teroldego, Sagrantino… You'll have to shell out up to a tenner for decent Chianti, more for Piedmont wines (especially Barolo and Barbaresco, so try Langhe instead). Valpolicella can be very good, but choose with care. Portugal reveals something of the same character in its reds.

- Chianti, plus other wines made from the Sangiovese grape
- Barolo, Barbaresco and other wines made from the Nebbiolo grape
- Valpolicella Classico, Amarone della Valpolicella
- Southern Italian reds
- Touriga Nacional and other Portuguese reds

Delicate (and not-so-delicate) rosé

Dry rosé can be wonderful, with flavours of strawberries and maybe raspberries and rosehips, cherries, apples and herbs, too. Look for wines made from sturdy grapes like Cabernet, Syrah or Merlot, or go for Grenache/Garnacha or Tempranillo from Spain and the Rhône Valley. South America is a good bet for flavoursome, fruit-forward pink wine. *See pages 103–7 for my top pinks this year.*

Drink organic – or even biodynamic

- The widely discussed benefits of organic farming – respect for the environment, minimal chemical residues in our food and drink – apply to grapes as much as to any other produce. Full-blown organic viticulture forbids the use of synthetic fertilizers, herbicides or fungicides; instead, cover crops and companion planting encourage biodiversity and natural predators to keep the soil and vines healthy. Warm, dry climates like the South of France, Chile and South Africa have the advantage of rarely suffering from the damp that can cause rot, mildew and other problems – we should be seeing more organic wines from these regions. Organic wines from European countries are often labelled 'Biologique', or simply 'Bio'.

- Biodynamic viticulture takes working with nature one stage further: work in the vineyard is planned in accordance with the movements of the planets, moon, sun and cosmic forces to achieve health and balance in the soil and in the vine. Vines are treated with infusions of mineral, animal and plant materials, applied in homeopathic quantities, with some astonishing results.

- If you want to know more, the best companies to contact are Vinceremos and Vintage Roots (see page 187).

Sparkling wines

Champagne can be the finest sparkling wine on the planet, but fizz made by the traditional Champagne method in Australia, New Zealand or California – often using the same grape varieties – is often just as good and cheaper. It might be a little more fruity, where Champagne concentrates on bready, yeasty or nutty aromas, but a few are dead ringers for the classic style. Fizz is also made in other parts of France: Crémant de Bourgogne is one of the best. England is beginning to show its potential. Italy's Prosecco is soft and delicately scented. Spain's Cava is perfect party fizz available at bargain basement prices in all the big supermarkets.

• Champagne
• Traditional method fizz made from Chardonnay, Pinot Noir and Pinot Meunier grapes grown in Australia, California, England, New Zealand, South Africa
• Crémant de Bourgogne, Crémant de Loire, Crémant de Jura, Crémant d'Alsace, Blanquette de Limoux
• Cava
• Prosecco
• Sekt is Germany's sparkling wine, and is occasionally 100 per cent Riesling
• Lambrusco from Italy is gently sparkling and usually red
• Sparkling Shiraz – an Aussie speciality – will make a splash at a wild party

Fortified wines

Tangy, appetizing fortified wines

To set your taste buds tingling, fino and manzanilla sherries are pale, perfumed, bone dry and bracingly tangy. True amontillado, dark and nutty, is also dry. Dry oloroso adds deep, raisiny flavours. Palo cortado falls between amontillado and oloroso; manzanilla pasada is an older, nuttier manzanilla. The driest style of Madeira, Sercial, is steely and smoky; Verdelho Madeira is a bit fuller and richer, but still tangy and dry.

• Manzanilla and fino sherry

• Dry amontillado, palo cortado and dry oloroso sherry

• Sercial and Verdelho Madeira

Rich, warming fortified wines

Raisins and brown sugar, dried figs and caramelized nuts – do you like the sound of that? Port is the classic dark sweet wine, and it comes in several styles, from basic ruby, to tawny, matured in cask for 10 years or more, to vintage, which matures to mellowness in the bottle. The Portuguese island of Madeira produces fortified wines with rich brown smoky flavours and a startling bite of acidity: the sweet styles to look for are Bual and Malmsey. Decent sweet sherries are rare; oloroso dulce is a style with stunningly concentrated flavours. In southern France, Banyuls and Maury are deeply fruity fortified wines. Marsala, from Sicily, has rich brown sugar flavours with a refreshing sliver of acidity. The versatile Muscat grape makes luscious golden wines all around the Mediterranean, but also pops up in orange, black, and the gloriously rich, treacly brown versions that Australia does superbly.

• Port

• Bual and Malmsey Madeira

• Marsala

• Rich, sweet sherry styles include Pedro Ximénez, oloroso dulce

• Vins doux naturels from southern France: Banyuls, Maury

• Fortified (liqueur) Muscat 'stickies' from Australia

Buying wine for the long term

Most of this book is about wines to drink more or less immediately – that's how modern wines are made, and that's what you'll find in most high street retail outlets. If you're looking for a mature vintage of a great wine that's ready to drink – or are prepared to wait 10 years or more for a great vintage to reach its peak – specialist wine merchants will be able to help; the internet's another good place to look for mature wines. Here's my beginners' guide to buying wine for drinking over the longer term.

Auctions

A wine sale catalogue from one of the UK's auction houses will have wine enthusiasts drooling over names they certainly don't see every day. Better still, the lots are often of mature vintages that are ready to drink. Before you go, find out all you can about the producer and vintages described in the catalogue. My annually updated *Pocket Wine Book* is a good place to start, or *Michael Broadbent's Vintage Wines* for old and rare wines; *Decanter*, the national wine magazine, runs regular features on wine regions and their vintages. You can also learn a lot from tutored tastings – especially 'vertical' tastings, which compare different vintages. This is important – some merchants take the opportunity to clear inferior vintages at auction.

The drawbacks? You have no guarantee that the wine has been well stored, and if it's faulty you have little chance of redress. As prices of the most sought-after wines have soared, so it has become profitable either to forge the bottles and their contents or to try to pass off stock that is clearly out of condition. But for expensive and mature wines, I have to say that the top auction houses make a considerable effort to check the provenance and integrity of the wines. Don't forget that there will usually be a commission or buyers' premium to pay, so check out the small print in the sale catalogue. Online wine auctions have similar pros and cons.

If you've never bought wine at an auction before, a good place to start would be a local auctioneer such as Straker Chadwick in Abergavenny (tel: 01873 852624, www.strakerchadwick.co.uk) or Morphets in Harrogate (tel: 01423 530030, www.morphets.co.uk); they're less intimidating than the famous London houses of Christie's and Sotheby's and you may come away with some really exciting wine.

Buying en primeur

En primeur is a French term for wine which is sold before it is bottled, sometimes referred to as a 'future'. In the spring after the vintage, the Bordeaux châteaux – and a few other wine-producing regions, particularly Burgundy and the Rhône in good vintages – hold tastings of barrel samples for members of the international wine trade. The châteaux then offer a proportion of their production to the wine merchants (*négociants*) in Bordeaux, who in turn offer it to wine merchants around the world at an opening price.

The advantage to the châteaux is that their capital is not tied up in expensive stock for the next year or two, until the wines are bottled and ready to ship. Traditionally merchants would buy en primeur for stock to be sold later at a higher price, while offering their customers the chance to take advantage of the opening prices as well. The idea of private individuals investing rather than institutions took off with a series of good Bordeaux vintages in the 1980s; it's got ever more hectic since then.

Wine for the future

There is a lot to be said for buying en primeur. For one thing, in a great vintage you may be able to find the finest and rarest wines far more cheaply than they will ever appear again. Every classic vintage in Bordeaux opens at a higher and higher price, but that price never permanently drops, and so the top wines increase in value, whatever price they start at. Equally, when a wine – even a relatively inexpensive one – is made in very limited quantities, buying en primeur may be practically your only chance of getting hold of it.

In the past, British wine merchants and their privileged customers were able to 'buy double what you want, sell half for double what you paid, and drink for free', but as the market has opened up to people more interested in making a quick buck than drinking fine wine, the whole process has become more risky.

Another potential hazard is that a tasting assessment is difficult at an early date. There is a well-founded suspicion that many barrel samples are doctored (legally) to appeal to the most powerful consumer critics, in particular the American Robert Parker and the *Wine Spectator* magazine. The wine that is finally bottled may or may not bear a resemblance to what was tasted in the spring following the vintage. In any case, most serious red wines are in a difficult stage of their evolution in the spring, and with the best will in the world it is possible to get one's evaluation wrong. However, the aforementioned Americans, and magazines like *Decanter* and the broadsheet newspapers, will do their best to offer you accurate judgements on the newly offered wines, and most merchants who make a primeur offer also write a good assessment of the wines. You will find that many of them quote the Parker or *Wine Spectator* marks. Anything over 90 out of 100 risks being hyped and hiked in price. Many of the best bargains get marks between 85 and 89, since the 90+ marks are generally awarded for power rather than subtlety. Consideration can be given to the producer's reputation for consistency and to the general vintage assessment for the region.

Bordeaux swings and roundabouts

Prices can go down as well as up. They may not increase significantly for some years after the en primeur campaign. Some popular vintages are offered at ridiculously high prices – some unpopular ones too. It's only about twice a decade that the combination of high quality and fair prices offers the private buyer a chance of a good, guaranteed profit. Interestingly, if one highly-touted vintage is followed by another, the prices for the second one often have to fall because the market simply will not accept two inflated price structures in a row. Recent Bordeaux examples of this are the excellent 2004 after the much-hyped 2003 and the fine 2001 after the understandably hyped 2000. Sadly this message didn't get through in 2005 and 2006. Opening prices for 2005 were as much as 400% up on 2004 for the top wines. The unexciting 2006s dropped by a mere 15% from 2005's vastly inflated level.

But the point to remember is that these crazy headline prices are for the top wines. Modern Bordeaux makes more and more good red each year, and the prices rise modestly, if at all. So while top 2006s might rise by £1,000 a year per case, the vast majority, not overpraised by critics or craved by the affluent new Asian markets, have hardly moved, except for enforced changes due to a weak pound. But I'm afraid an awful lot of wine in the hyper-hyped 2009 vintage is going to be overpriced. Merchants are reporting that ten times as many people as usual are trying to buy the 2009 wines – and they're not even in bottle yet. Most properties haven't even made their final blends. In the fabled 2005 vintage, top wines were released for about £3,000 per case of 12. Long before the Big Boys said what their prices for 2009 would be, wines like Chateau Lafite were being touted for £13,000 a case. So what do you do? Either wait – a lot of the less glamorous 2005s haven't really risen in price in the past four years – or buy 2008s. Although 2006 and 2007 weren't generally exciting, 2008s are delightfully fragrant and attractive, and much cheaper than 2009.

Secure cellarage

Another worry is that the merchant you buy the wine from may not still be around to deliver it to you two years later. Buy from a well-established merchant you trust, with a solid trading base in other wines.

Once the wines are shipped you may want your merchant to store the wine for you; there is usually a small charge for this. If your merchant offers cellarage, you should insist that (1) you receive a stock certificate; (2) your wines are stored separately from the merchant's own stocks; and (3) your cases are identifiable as your property. All good merchants offer these safeguards as a minimum service.

Check the small print

Traditional wine merchants may quote prices exclusive of VAT and/or duty: wine may not be the bargain it first appears. A wine quoted en primeur is usually offered on an ex-cellars (EC) basis; the price excludes shipping, duties and taxes such as VAT. A price quoted in bond (IB) in the UK includes shipping, but excludes duties and taxes. Duty paid (DP) prices exclude VAT. You should check beforehand the exact terms of sale with your merchant, who will give you a projection of the final 'duty paid delivered' price.

Retailers' directory

All these retailers have been chosen on the basis of the quality and interest of their lists. If you want to find a local retailer, turn to the Who's Where directory on page 192. Case = 12 bottles

The following services are available where indicated:
C = cellarage   **G** = glass hire/loan   **M** = mail/online order   **T** = tastings and talks

A & B Vintners

Little Tawsden, Spout Lane, Brenchley, Kent TN12 7AS (01892) 724977 fax (01892) 722673
e-mail info@abvintners.co.uk website www.abvintners.co.uk hours Mon–Fri 9–6 cards MasterCard, Visa
delivery 1–4 cases £12 + VAT within M25; £17 Home Counties; free for 5 cases or more within these areas; phone for
information on other areas minimum order 1 mixed case en primeur Burgundy, Languedoc, Rhône. C M T
✪ *Specialists in Burgundy, the Rhône and southern France, with a string of top-quality domaines from all three regions.*

Adnams

head office & mail order Sole Bay Brewery, Southwold, Suffolk IP18 6JW (01502) 727222 fax (01502) 727223
e-mail customerservices@adnams.co.uk website www.adnams.co.uk hours (Orderline) Mon–Fri 9–5.30; see also shops
shops • Adnams Wine Shop, Pinkney's Lane, Southwold, Suffolk IP18 6EW Mon–Sat 9.30–5.30, Sun 10–4 • Adnams Cellar
& Kitchen Store, 4 Drayman Square, Southwold, Suffolk IP18 6GB Mon–Sat 9–6, Sun 10–4 • The Old School House, Park
Road, Holkham, Wells-next-the-Sea, Norfolk NR23 1AB (01328) 711714 Mon–Sat 10–6, Sun 11–4 • Station Road,
Woodbridge, Suffolk IP12 4AU (01394) 386594 Mon–Sat 10–6, Sun 11–4 • Bath Row Warehouse, St Mary's Passage,
Stamford, Lincolnshire PE9 2HG (01780) 753127 Mon–Sat 10–6, Sun 11–4 • The Cardinal's Hat, 23 The Thoroughfare,
Harleston, Norfolk IP20 9AS (01379) 854788 Mon–Sat 10–6 • 1 Market Street, Saffron Walden, Essex CB10 1JB (01799)
527281 Mon–Sat 9–6 • 23a Lees Yard, Off Bull Street, Holt, Norfolk NR25 6HS (01263) 715558 Mon– Sat 9–6
• 73–75 High Street, Hadleigh, Suffolk IP7 5DY (01473) 827796 Mon–Sat 9–6 • 26 Hill Rise, Richmond-upon-Thames,
Surrey TW10 6UA (020) 8940 8684 Mon–Sat 9–6, Sun 11–5 cards AmEx, Maestro, MasterCard, Visa, Delta delivery Free
for orders over £50 in most of mainland UK, otherwise £7.50 en primeur Bordeaux, Burgundy, Chile, Rhône. G M T
✪ *Extensive list of personality-packed wines from around the world, chosen by Adnams' enthusiastic team of buyers.*

Aldi Stores

head office Holly Lane, Atherstone CV9 2SQ; over 400 stores in the UK customer service 0844 406 8800 website www.aldi.co.uk hours Mon–Fri 9–8, Sat 8.30–8, Sun 10–4 (selected stores; check website) cards Maestro, MasterCard, Visa Debit, Solo.
✪ *Decent everyday stuff from around the world, with lots of wines under £4.*

armit

mail order/online 5 Royalty Studios, 105 Lancaster Road, London W11 1QF (020) 7908 0600 fax (020) 7908 0601 e-mail info@armit.co.uk website www.armit.co.uk hours Mon–Fri 8.45–5.15 cards Maestro, MasterCard, Visa delivery Free over £250, otherwise £15 delivery charge minimum order 1 case en primeur Bordeaux, Burgundy, Italy, Rhône, New World. C M T
✪ *Particularly strong on wines to go with food – they supply some of the country's top restaurants.*

ASDA

head office Asda House, Southbank, Great Wilson Street, Leeds LS11 5AD (0113) 243 5435 customer service (0500) 100055; 367 stores website www.asda.co.uk hours Selected stores open 24 hours, see local store for details cards Maestro, MasterCard, Visa.
✪ *Large and increasingly exciting range of great-value wines at all price points, selected by Philippa Carr MW.*

AustralianWineCentre.co.uk

mail order/online PO Box 3854, Datchet, Slough SL3 3EN 0800 756 1141 fax (01753) 208040 email customerservice@AustralianWineCentre.co.uk website www.AustralianWineCentre.co.uk cards MasterCard, Visa delivery Free for orders over £100, otherwise £5 per order; UK mainland only minimum order 12 bottles.
✪ *The original Aussie specialist with some brilliant Australian wines.*

Averys Wine Merchants

head office 4 High Street, Nailsea, Bristol BS48 1BT 0843 224 1224 fax (01275) 811101 e-mail sales@averys.com website www.averys.com • Shop and Cellars, 9 Culver Street, Bristol BS1 5LD (0117) 921 4146 fax (0117) 922 6318 e-mail cellars@averys.com hours Mon–Fri 8–8, Sat–Sun 9–6; Shop Mon–Sat 10–7 cards Maestro, MasterCard, Visa delivery £6.99 per delivery address en primeur Bordeaux, Burgundy, Port, Rhône. C G M T
✪ *A small but very respectable selection from just about everywhere in France, Italy and Spain, as well as some good stuff from New Zealand, Australia and Chile.*

Ballantynes Wine Merchants

211–217 Cathedral Road, Cardiff CF11 9PP (02920) 222202 fax (02920) 222112 e-mail richard@ballantynes.co.uk website www.ballantynes-direct.co.uk hours Mon–Fri 9.30–6.30, Sat 9.30–5.30 cards Access, Maestro, MasterCard, Visa discounts 8% per case for local delivery or collection delivery Free for orders over £100; otherwise £10.99 minimum order £50 (mail order) en primeur Bordeaux, Burgundy, Italy, Rhône. C G M T
✪ *Most regions of France are well represented; Italy, Spain and Portugal look good; and Australia and New Zealand are particularly tempting.*

Balls Brothers

313 Cambridge Heath Road, London E2 9LQ (020) 7739 1642 fax 0870 243 9775 direct sales (020) 7739 1642 e-mail wine@ballsbrothers.co.uk website www.ballsbrothers.co.uk hours Mon–Fri 9–5.30 cards AmEx, Maestro, MasterCard, Visa delivery Free 1 case or more locally; £10 for 1 case or free for orders over £175 in England, Wales and Scottish Lowlands; islands and Scottish Highlands, phone for details. G M T
✪ *French specialist – you'll find something of interest from most regions – with older vintages available. Spain and Australia are also very good. Many of the wines can be enjoyed in Balls Brothers' London wine bars and restaurants.*

Bancroft Wines

mail order Woolyard, 54 Bermondsey Street, London SE1 3UD (020) 7232 5440 fax (020) 7232 5451 e-mail sales@bancroftwines.com website www.bancroftwines.com hours Mon–Fri 9–5.30 cards Delta, Maestro, MasterCard, Visa discounts Negotiable delivery £15 for 1–2 cases in mainland UK; free 3 cases or more or for orders of £350 or more minimum order 1 mixed case en primeur Bordeaux, Burgundy, Rhône. C M T
✪ *Bancroft are UK agents for an impressive flotilla of French winemakers: Burgundy, Rhône, Loire and some interesting wines from southern France. There is plenty of New World, too.*

Bat & Bottle

Unit 5, 19 Pillings Road, Oakham LE15 6QF (01572) 759735 e-mail ben@batwine.co.uk website www.batwine.co.uk hours Mon–Fri 10–4, Sat 9–2; ring or check website before visiting cards Maestro, MasterCard, Visa delivery Free for orders over £150. G M T
• Ben's Wine Shop, 10 Northgate, Oakham, Rutland LE15 6QS (01572) 759735 hours Wed 9–1, Fri 10–7, Sat 9–1
✪ *Ben and Emma Robson specialize in Italy, and in characterful wines from small producers. They also sell a few favourites from elsewhere, too.*

Bennetts Fine Wines

High Street, Chipping Campden, Glos GL55 6AG (01386) 840392 fax (01386) 840974 hours Mon–Sat 9.30–6
• Edward Sheldon, New Street, Shipston-on-Stour, Warwickshire CV36 4EN (01608) 661409 fax (01608) 663166
hours Mon–Wed 9–6, Thur–Fri 9–7, Sat 9.30–6 e-mail shop@bennettsfinewines.com
website www.bennettsfinewines.com cards Access, Maestro, MasterCard, Visa discounts On collected orders of 1 case
or more delivery £6 per case, minimum charge £12, free for orders over £200 en primeur Burgundy, California, New
Zealand, Rhône. G M T
✪ *Reasonable prices for high-calibre producers – there's lots to choose from at around £10. Mainly from France and Italy,
but some good German, Spanish and Portuguese wines, too.*

Berkmann Wine Cellars

10–12 Brewery Road, London N7 9NH (020) 7609 4711 fax (020) 7607 0018 e-mail orders@berkmann.co.uk
• Brunel Park, Vincients Road, Bumpers Farm, Chippenham, Wiltshire SN14 6NQ (01249) 463501
fax (01249) 463502 e-mail orders.chippenham@berkmann.co.uk
• Churchill Vintners, 401 Walsall Road, Perry Bar, Birmingham B42 1BT (0121) 356 8888
fax (0121) 356 1111 e-mail sales@churchill-vintners.co.uk
• Coad Wine Cellars, 41b Valley Road, Plympton, Plymouth, Devon PL7 1RF (01752) 334970
fax (01752) 346540 e-mail orders.briancoad@berkmann.co.uk
• Pagendam Pratt Wine Cellars, 16 Marston Moor Business Park, Rudgate, Tockwith, North Yorkshire YO26 7QF
(01423) 357567 fax (01423) 357568 e-mail orders@pagendampratt.co.uk
website www.berkmann.co.uk hours Mon–Fri 9–5.30 cards Maestro, MasterCard, Visa discounts £3 per unmixed case
collected delivery Free for orders over £120 to UK mainland (excluding the Highlands) minimum order 1 mixed case. C M
✪ *UK agent for, among others, Antinori, Casa Lapostolle, Chapel Hill, Deutz, Duboeuf, Mastroberardino, Masi, Norton, Rioja
Alta and Tasca d'Almerita. An incredibly diverse list, with some great Italian wines.*

Berry Bros. & Rudd

3 St James's Street, London SW1A 1EG 0800 280 2440 hours Mon–Fri 10–6, Sat 10–5
sales and services 0800 280 2440 (lines open Mon–Fri 9–6) fax 0800 280 2443
e-mail bbr@bbr.com website www.bbr.com cards AmEx, Diners, Maestro, MasterCard, Visa discounts Variable
delivery Free for orders of £200 or more, otherwise £10 en primeur Bordeaux, Burgundy, Rhône. C G M T
• Berrys' Factory Outlet, Hamilton Close, Houndmills, Basingstoke, Hampshire RG21 6YB 0800 280 2440
hours Mon–Fri 10–6, Sat–Sun 10–4

✪ *Classy and wide-ranging list. There's an emphasis on the classic regions of France. Berry's Own Selection is extensive, with wines made by world-class producers.*

Bibendum Wine

mail order 113 Regents Park Road, London NW1 8UR (020) 7449 4120 **fax** (020) 7449 4121
e-mail sales@bibendum-wine.co.uk **website** www.bibendum-wine.co.uk **hours** Mon–Fri 9–6
cards Maestro, MasterCard, Visa **delivery** Free throughout mainland UK for orders over £350, otherwise £15
en primeur Bordeaux, Burgundy, New World, Rhône, Port. M T
✪ *Equally strong in the Old World and the New: Huet in Vouvray and Lageder in Alto Adige are matched by d'Arenberg and Katnook from Australia and Catena Zapata from Argentina.*

Big Red Wine Company

mail order Barton Coach House, The Street, Barton Mills, Suffolk IP28 6AA (01638) 510803
e-mail sales@bigredwine.co.uk **website** www.bigredwine.co.uk **hours** Mon–Sat 9–6 **cards** AmEx, Delta, Maestro,
MasterCard, Visa, PayPal **discounts** 5–15% for Wine Club members; negotiable for large orders
delivery £7 per consignment for orders under £200, £10 for orders under £50, UK mainland
en primeur Bordeaux, Rhône, South-West France. C G M T
✪ *Intelligently chosen, reliably individualistic wines from good estates in France, Italy and Spain. A list worth reading, full of information and provocative opinion – and they're not overcharging.*

Booths

central office Longridge Road, Ribbleton, Preston PR2 5BX (01772) 693800; 26 stores across the North of England
fax (01772) 693893 **website** www.everywine.co.uk, www.booths.co.uk **hours** Office: Mon–Fri 8.30–5; shop hours vary
cards AmEx, Electron, Maestro, MasterCard, Solo, Visa **discounts** 5% off any 6 bottles. T
✪ *A list for any merchant to be proud of, never mind a supermarket. There's plenty around £5, but if you're prepared to hand over £7–9 you'll find some really interesting stuff.*

Bordeaux Index

mail order/online 10 Hatton Garden, London EC1N 8AH (020) 7269 0700 **fax** (020) 7269 0701
e-mail sales@bordeauxindex.com **website** www.bordeauxindex.com **hours** Mon–Fri 8.30–6 **cards** AmEx, Maestro,
MasterCard, Visa **delivery** (Private sales only) free for orders over £2000 UK mainland; visit the website for other delivery
details, including international **minimum order** £500 **en primeur** Bordeaux, Burgundy, Rhône, Italy. C M T

✪ *Extensive list of fine wines, including older vintages, focused on the classic regions of France and Italy, but with interesting stuff from elsewhere.*

Budgens Stores

head office Musgrave House, Widewater Place, Moorhall Road, Harefield, Uxbridge, Middlesex UB9 6NS 0870 050 0158 fax 0870 050 0159; 190 stores mainly in southern England and East Anglia – for nearest store call 0800 526002 website www.budgens.co.uk hours Variable; usually Mon–Sat 8–8, Sun 10–4 cards Maestro, MasterCard, Solo, Visa.
✪ *These days you can be reasonably confident of going into Budgens and coming out with something you'd really like to drink.*

The Butlers Wine Cellar

247 Queens Park Road, Brighton BN2 9XJ (01273) 698724 fax (01273) 622761 e-mail henry@butlers-winecellar.co.uk website www.butlers-winecellar.co.uk hours Mon–Wed, Fri 11–7, Thur, Sat 11–8, Sun 12–6 cards Access, AmEx, Maestro, MasterCard, Visa delivery Free nationally over £150 en primeur Bordeaux. G M T
✪ *Henry Butler personally chooses the wines and there is some fascinating stuff here, including English wines from local growers such as Breaky Bottom and Ridgeview. Check the website or join the mailing list as offers change regularly.*

Anthony Byrne Fine Wines

mail order Ramsey Business Park, Stocking Fen Road, Ramsey, Cambs PE26 2UR (01487) 814555 fax (01487) 814962 e-mail anthony@abfw.co.uk or gary@abfw.co.uk website www.abfw.co.uk hours Mon–Fri 9–5.30 cards MasterCard, Visa discounts Available on cases delivery Free 5 cases or more, or orders of £250 or more; otherwise £15 minimum order 1 case en primeur Bordeaux, Burgundy, Rhône. C M T
✪ *A serious range of Burgundy; smaller but focused lists from Bordeaux and the Rhône; carefully selected wines from Alsace, Loire and Provence; and a wide range of New World.*

D Byrne & Co

Victoria Buildings, 12 King Street, Clitheroe, Lancashire BB7 2EP (01200) 423152 website www.dbyrne-finewines.co.uk hours Mon–Sat 8.30–6 cards Maestro, MasterCard, Visa delivery Free within 40 miles; nationally £10 1st case, further cases additional £2.50 en primeur Bordeaux, Burgundy, Rhône, Germany. G M T
✪ *A family business since the 1870s and one of northern England's best wine merchants. A hugely impressive range of wines, as well as over 300 malt whiskies and over 30 vodkas. I urge you to go and see for yourself.*

The following services are available where indicated: C = cellarage **G** = glass hire/loan **M** = mail/online order **T** = tastings and talks

Cambridge Wine Merchants

head office 29 Dry Drayton Industries, Scotland Road, Dry Drayton CB23 8AT (01954) 214528 fax (01954) 214574
e-mail cambridgewine@cambridgewine.com website www.cambridgewine.com
- 42 Mill Road, Cambridge CB1 2AD (01223) 568993 e-mail mill@cambridgewine.com
- 32 Bridge Street, Cambridge CB2 1UJ (01223) 568989 e-mail bridge@cambridgewine.com
- 2 King's Parade, Cambridge CB2 1SJ (01223) 309309 e-mail kings@cambridgewine.com
- 163 Cherry Hinton Road, Cambridge CB1 7BX (01223) 214548 e-mail cherry@cambridgewine.com
- 12 Church Street, Ampthill MK45 2PL (01525) 405929 e-mail ampthill@cambridgewine.com
- 34b Kneesworth Street, Royston SG8 5AB (01763) 247076 e-mail royston@cambridgewine.com
- Edinburgh Wine Merchants, 30b Raeburn Place, Edinburgh EH4 IHN (0131) 343 2347

e-mail stockbridge@edinburghwine.com hours Mon–Sat 10am–9pm, Sun 12–8 cards Amex, MasterCard, Switch, Visa
discounts Buy 4 bottles, get the cheapest one free (selected lines) delivery Free for 12 bottles or more within 5 miles of
Cambridge; £2.50 for less than 12 bottles. National delivery £6.50 per case of 12 bottles; £9.99 for 1 to 11 bottles
en primeur Bordeaux, Burgundy, Rhône, Port. C G M T
✪ *Young, unstuffy merchants with a well-chosen list: no dross, just a tight focus on good, individual producers, with
particularly interesting Australian, German, Champagne and dessert sections. They're also very serious about port –
as befits their university roots. Informative monthly newsletter. Every branch has a wine tasting club.*

Les Caves de Pyrène

Pew Corner, Old Portsmouth Road, Artington, Guildford GU3 1LP (office) (01483) 538820 (shop) (01483) 554750
fax (01483) 455068 e-mail sales@lescaves.co.uk website www.lescaves.co.uk hours Mon–Fri 9–5
cards Maestro, MasterCard, Visa delivery Free for orders over £180 within London, elsewhere at cost
discounts Negotiable minimum order 1 mixed case en primeur South-West France. G M T
✪ *Excellent operation, devoted to seeking out top wines from all over southern France. Other areas of France are looking
increasingly good too, Italy's regions are well represented, and there's some choice stuff from New Zealand.*

ChateauOnline

mail order 39 rue du Général Foy, 75008 Paris, France (00 33) 1 55 30 30 27 fax (00 33) 1 55 30 30 63
sales 0800 169 2736 website www.chateauonline.com hours Mon–Thur 8–5, Fri 8–4 cards AmEx, Maestro,
MasterCard, Visa, PayPal delivery £14.99 per consignment, free for orders over £100 en primeur Bordeaux, Burgundy.
✪ *French specialist, with an impressive list of around 1500 wines. Easy-to-use website with a well-thought-out
range of mixed cases, frequent special offers and bin end sales.*

Chilean Wine Club

online c/o Pinewood Nurseries, Wexham Street, Stoke Poges, Buckinghamshire SL3 6NB (01753) 664190
e-mail info@chileanwineclub.co.uk website www.chileanwineclub.co.uk cards AmEx, Delta, Maestro, MasterCard, Visa
delivery £6.99 per address; free for orders over £250 in UK mainland; free to postcode SL9 irrespective of number
of cases minimum order 1 mixed case.
✪ *Come here to find many of Chile's finest wines that are not available on the high street – Errázuriz, Tabalí and Emiliana,
South America's largest organic producer, are three excellent names from the list. Under the same ownership as The Real
Wine Company (see page 180).*

Cockburns of Leith

mail order/online Thistle House, Caputhall Road, Deans Industrial Estate, Livingston EH54 8AS (01506) 468 900
fax (01506) 414 486 e-mail imacphail-cockburns@wine-importers.net website www.cockburnsofleith.co.uk
hours Mon–Fri 9–5 cards Maestro, MasterCard, Visa delivery Free 12 or more bottles within Edinburgh; elsewhere
£9.99 en primeur Bordeaux, Burgundy. M
✪ *Scotland's oldest surviving wine merchant, founded in 1796; under new ownership since 2010. Most major wine regions
covered. Older vintages of Bordeaux, Burgundy and the Rhône.*

Colchester Wine Company

Gosbecks Park, Colchester, Essex CO2 9JT (01206) 713560 fax (01206) 713515 e-mail sales@thewinecompany.co.uk
website www.thewinecompany.co.uk hours Mon–Sat 9–6 cards Delta, Electron, MasterCard, Maestro, Switch, Visa
delivery £7.99 or free for orders over £200 within UK mainland; please ring or email for quote for Highlands, islands and
Northern Ireland. C G M T
✪ *Family-owned wine merchant, strong in French wines and wines from smaller estates, with plenty under £10.
Well-chosen mixed case offers and regular tastings and dinners.*

Connolly's Wine Merchants

Arch 13, 220 Livery Street, Birmingham B3 1EU (0121) 236 9269/3837 fax (0121) 233 2339
website www.connollyswine.co.uk hours Mon–Fri 9–5.30, Sat 10–4 cards AmEx, Maestro, MasterCard, Visa
delivery Surcharge outside Birmingham area discounts 10% for cash & carry en primeur Burgundy. G M T
✪ *Award-winning merchant that has something for everyone. Burgundy, Bordeaux and the Rhône all look very good; and
there are top names from Germany, Italy, Spain and California. Weekly in-store tastings, monthly tutored tastings and
winemaker dinners. Birmingham's largest whisky retailer, too.*

The Co-operative Group (Co-op)

head office New Century House, Manchester M60 4ES Freephone 0800 0686 727 for stock details; approx. 3200 licensed stores e-mail customer.relations@co-op.co.uk website www.co-operative.coop hours Variable cards Variable.

✪ *Champions of Fairtrade, with wines from South Africa, Argentina and Chile. Tasty stuff from around £5 and some real finds at £7–10. A small list of fine wines between £10 and £20 available in premium stores. The Co-operative Group bought the Somerfield chain in 2009 and is in the process of rebranding stores.*

Corney & Barrow

head office No. 1 Thomas More Street, London E1W 1YZ (020) 7265 2400 fax (020) 7265 2539 hours Mon–Fri 8–6 (24-hr answering machine) e-mail wine@corneyandbarrow.com website www.corneyandbarrow.com

• Corney & Barrow East Anglia, Belvoir House, High Street, Newmarket CB8 8DH (01638) 600000 hours Mon–Sat 9–6

• Corney & Barrow (Scotland) with Whighams of Ayr, 8 Academy Street, Ayr KA7 1HT (01292) 267000 hours Mon–Sat 10–5.30

• Oxenfoord Castle, by Pathhead, Mid Lothian EH37 5UD (01875) 321921 hours Mon–Fri 9–6 cards AmEx, Maestro, MasterCard, Visa delivery Free for all orders above £200 within mainland UK, otherwise £12.50 per delivery. For Scotland and East Anglia, please contact the relevant office en primeur Bordeaux, Burgundy, Champagne, Rhône, Italy, Spain. C G M T

✪ *Top names in French and other European wines; Australia, South Africa and South America are also impressive. Wines in every price bracket – try them out at Corney & Barrow wine bars in London.*

Croque-en-Bouche

mail order Old Post Office Cottage, Putley Green, Ledbury, Herefordshire HR8 2QN (01531) 670809 fax 08707 066282 e-mail mail@croque-en-bouche.co.uk website www.croque-en-bouche.co.uk hours By appointment 7 days a week cards MasterCard, Visa, debit cards discounts 3% for orders over £500 if paid by cheque or debit card delivery Free locally; elsewhere in England and Wales £5 per order; free in England and Wales for orders over £500 if paid by credit card; please ring or email for quote for Highlands, islands, Northern Ireland and elsewhere minimum order 1 mixed case (12 items) or £180. M

✪ *A wonderful list, including older wines. Mature Australian reds from the 1990s; terrific stuff from the Rhône; some top clarets; and a generous sprinkling from other parts of the world.*

DeFINE Food & Wine

Chester Road, Sandiway, Cheshire CW8 2NH (01606) 882101 fax (01606) 888407

e-mail office@definefoodandwine.com website www.definefoodandwine.com
hours Mon–Thur 10–7, Fri–Sat 10–8, Sun 12–6 cards AmEx, Maestro, MasterCard, Visa
discounts 5% off 12 bottles or more delivery Free locally, otherwise £7.50 UK. C G M T
✪ *Wine shop and delicatessen, with British cheeses and many food specialities from Italy and Spain. Excellent, wide-ranging list of over 1000 wines including a strong line-up from Argentina, New Zealand and South Africa, as well as European classics.*

Devigne Wines

mail order PO Box 13748, North Berwick EH39 9AA (01620) 890860 fax (05600) 756 287
e-mail info@devignewines.co.uk website www.devignewines.co.uk hours Mon–Fri 10–6 cards Maestro, MasterCard, Visa discounts Selected mixed cases at introductory rate delivery Free for orders over £300, otherwise £6.50 per consignment; please ring for quote for Highlands and islands. M
✪ *Small list specializing in French wine: traditional-method sparkling wines from all over France; a wide choice of rosés; Gaillac from the South-West; and wines from the Languedoc and the Jura.*

Direct Wine See Laithwaites.

Direct Wine Shipments

5–7 Corporation Square, Belfast, Northern Ireland BT1 3AJ (028) 9050 8000
fax (028) 9050 8004 e-mail shop@directwine.co.uk and info@directwine.co.uk website www.directwine.co.uk
hours Mon–Fri 9.30–7 (Thur 10–8), Sat 9.30–5.30 cards Delta, Electron, Maestro, MasterCard, Solo, Switch, Visa
discounts 10% in the form of complementary wine with each case delivery Free Northern Ireland 1 case or more, variable delivery charge for UK mainland depending on customer spend en primeur Bordeaux, Burgundy, Rhône. C M T
✪ *Rhône, Spain, Australia and Burgundy outstanding; Italy, Germany and Chile not far behind; there's good stuff from pretty much everywhere. Wine courses, tastings and expert advice offered.*

Nick Dobson Wines

mail order 38 Crail Close, Wokingham, Berkshire RG41 2PZ 0800 849 3078 fax 0870 460 2358
e-mail nick.dobson@nickdobsonwines.co.uk website www.nickdobsonwines.co.uk hours Mon–Sat 9–5
cards Access, Maestro, MasterCard, Visa delivery £8.95 + VAT 1 case; £7.95 + VAT 2nd and subsequent cases to UK mainland addresses. Free local delivery. M T
✪ *Specialist in wines from Switzerland, Austria and Beaujolais, plus intriguing selections from elsewhere in Europe.*

Domaine Direct

mail order 6–9 Cynthia Street, London N1 9JF (020) 7837 1142 fax (020) 7837 8605
e-mail mail@domainedirect.co.uk website www.domainedirect.co.uk hours Mon–Fri 8.30–6 or answering machine
cards Maestro, MasterCard, Visa delivery Free London; elsewhere in UK mainland 1 case £15, 2 cases £21, 3 cases
£23.50, 4 or more free and for all orders over £400 + VAT minimum order 1 mixed case
en primeur Burgundy (in top vintages). C M T
✪ *Sensational Burgundy list; prices are very reasonable for the quality. Also the Burgundian-style Chardonnays from Australia's Leeuwin Estate.*

Farr Vintners

mail order/online only 220 Queenstown Road, Battersea, London SW8 4LP (020) 7821 2000 fax (020) 7821 2020
e-mail sales@farrvintners.com website www.farrvintners.com hours Mon–Fri 9–6 cards Access, Maestro,
MasterCard, Visa delivery London £1 per case (min £15); elsewhere at cost minimum order £500 + VAT
en primeur Bordeaux. C M T
✪ *A fantastic list of the world's finest wines. The majority is Bordeaux, but you'll also find top stuff and older vintages of white Burgundy, red Rhône, plus Italy, Australia and California.*

Fingal-Rock

64 Monnow Street, Monmouth NP25 3EN tel & fax 01600 712372 e-mail tom@pinotnoir.co.uk
website www.pinotnoir.co.uk hours Mon 9.30–1.30, Thur & Fri 9.30–5.30, Sat 9.30–5 cards Maestro, MasterCard,
Visa discounts 5% for at least 12 bottles collected from shop, 7.5% for collected orders over £500, 10% for collected
orders over £1200 delivery Free locally (within 30 miles); orders further afield free if over £100. G M T
✪ *The website address gives you a clue that the list's great strength is Burgundy, especially reds. There are wines from some very good growers and at a range of prices between £8 and £40. Small but tempting selections from other French regions, as well as other parts of Europe and the New World and wines from local producer, Monnow Valley.*

Flagship Wines

417 Hatfield Road, St Albans, Hertfordshire AL4 0XP (01727) 865309 e-mail sales@flagshipwines.co.uk
website www.flagshipwines.co.uk hours Tues–Thur 11–6, Fri 11–7.30, Sat 10–6 cards Maestro, MasterCard, Visa
delivery Free to St Albans addresses and £10 to other UK mainland addresses. G M T
✪ *Independent whose prices can match those of the supermarkets – plus friendly, well-informed advice from boss Julia Jenkins. Strong in Australia, New Zealand, France and Spain but great stuff all round. Programme of tastings and events.*

The Flying Corkscrew

online only The Old Farm Bailiff's Office, Home Farm, Red Lion Lane, Great Gaddesden, Hertfordshire HP2 6EZ (01442) 213155 fax (01442) 215161 e-mail info@flyingcorkscrew.co.uk website www.flyingcorkscrew.co.uk hours Mon–Thur 10–7, Fri 10–8, Sat 10–6, Sun 11–4 cards AmEx, Maestro, MasterCard, Visa discounts 5% on 6 bottles, 15% on 12 bottles (mixed) delivery Free for orders over £150; £15 per case under £150. G M T
✪ *Extensive and imaginative range of wines from every corner of France. Italy, Australia and the US are terrific.*

Fortnum & Mason

181 Piccadilly, London W1A 1ER (020) 7734 8040 fax (020) 7437 3278 ordering line (020) 7973 4136 e-mail info@fortnumandmason.co.uk website www.fortnumandmason.com hours Mon–Sat 10–8, Sun 12–6 (Food Hall and Patio Restaurant only) cards AmEx, Diners, Maestro, MasterCard, Visa discounts 1 free bottle per unmixed dozen delivery £7 per delivery address en primeur Bordeaux. M T
✪ *Impressive names from just about everywhere, including Champagne, Bordeaux, Burgundy, Italy, Germany, Australia, New Zealand, South Africa and California. Impeccably sourced own-label range.*

Friarwood

26 New King's Road, London SW6 4ST (020) 7736 2628 fax (020) 7731 0411 e-mail simon.mckay@friarwood.com; christina@friarwood.com website www.friarwood.com
• 35 West Bowling Green Street, Edinburgh EH6 5NX (0131) 554 4159 fax (0131) 554 6703 e-mail edinburgh@friarwood.com
hours Mon–Sat 10–7 cards AmEx, Diners, Maestro, MasterCard, Visa, Solo, Electron discounts 5% on cases of 12 (mixed and unmixed) delivery (London) Free within M25 and on orders over £200 in mainland UK; (Edinburgh) free locally and on orders over £200 en primeur Bordeaux. C G M T
✪ *The focus is Bordeaux, including mature wines from a good selection of petits châteaux as well as classed growths. Burgundy and other French regions are strong, too.*

FromVineyardsDirect.com

online only Northburgh House, 10 Northburgh Street, London EC1V 0AT (020) 7490 9910 fax (020) 7490 3708 e-mail info@fromvineyardsdirect.com website www.fromvineyardsdirect.com hours 9–7 cards Maestro, MasterCard, Visa, Solo, Switch delivery Free minimum order 1 case (12 bottles) in UK mainland; 2 cases in Northern Ireland, Scottish Highlands and islands en primeur Bordeaux. C M T
✪ *A hand-picked selection of wines direct from vineyards in France, Italy and Spain, at very affordable prices.*

Gauntleys of Nottingham

4 High Street, Exchange Arcade, Nottingham NG1 2ET (0115) 911 0555 fax (0115) 911 0557 e-mail rhône@gauntleywine.com website www.gauntleywine.com hours Mon–Sat 9–5.30 cards Maestro, MasterCard, Visa delivery 1 case £11.95, 2–3 cases £9.95, 4 or more cases free minimum order 1 case en primeur Alsace, Burgundy, Loire, Rhône, southern France, Spain. M T

✪ *They've won countless awards for their Rhône and Alsace lists. The Loire, Burgundy, southern France and Spain are also excellent.*

Goedhuis & Co

6 Rudolf Place, Miles Street, London SW8 1RP (020) 7793 7900 fax (020) 7793 7170 e-mail sales@goedhuis.com website www.goedhuis.com hours Mon–Fri 9–5.30 cards Maestro, MasterCard, Visa delivery Free on orders over £250 ex-VAT; otherwise £15 ex-VAT England, elsewhere at cost minimum order 1 unmixed case en primeur Bordeaux, Burgundy, Rhône. C G M T

✪ *Fine wine specialist. Bordeaux, Burgundy and the Rhône are the core of the list, but everything is good. A sprinkling of New World producers, too.*

Great Northern Wine

The Warehouse, Blossomgate, Ripon, North Yorkshire HG4 2AJ (01765) 606767 fax (01765) 609151 e-mail info@greatnorthernwine.co.uk website www.greatnorthernwine.co.uk hours Tues–Wed 9–7, Thur–Sat 9–11 cards Maestro, MasterCard, Visa discounts 10% on case quantities delivery Free locally, elsewhere at cost en primeur Bordeaux. G M T

✪ *Independent shippers who seek out interesting wines from around the world. There's also a wine bar, where you can enjoy wines bought in the shop (£5 corkage charge).*

Great Western Wine

Wells Road, Bath BA2 3AP (01225) 322810 (enquiries) or (01225) 322820 (orders) fax (01225) 442139 e-mail orders@greatwesternwine.co.uk website www.greatwesternwine.co.uk hours Mon–Fri 10–7, Sat 10–6 cards AmEx, Maestro, MasterCard, Visa discounts 5% off mixed cases, 8% off unsplit cases delivery Free for 12 bottles or more in UK mainland; £8.95 for smaller orders en primeur Australia, Bordeaux, Burgundy, Rioja. C G M T

✪ *Wide-ranging list, bringing in brilliant wines from individual growers around the world. Also organizes events and tastings.*

The following services are available where indicated: C = cellarage **G** = glass hire/loan **M** = mail/online order **T** = tastings and talks

Peter Green & Co

37A/B Warrender Park Road, Edinburgh EH9 1HJ (0131) 229 5925 e-mail shop@petergreenwines.com
website www.petergreenwines.co.uk hours Tues–Thur 10–6.30, Fri 10–7.30, Sat 10–6.30 cards Maestro, MasterCard,
Visa discounts 5% on unmixed half-dozens delivery Free in Edinburgh minimum order (For delivery) 1 case. G T
❂ *Extensive and adventurous list: Tunisia, India and the Lebanon rub shoulders with the more classic countries.*

Green & Blue

36–38 Lordship Lane, East Dulwich, London SE22 8HJ (020) 8693 9250 e-mail info@greenandbluewines.com website
www.greenandbluewines.com hours Mon–Wed 9–11, Thur–Sat 9–midnight, Sun 11–10
cards Delta, Maestro, MasterCard, Visa discounts 5% off mixed cases of 12 (collection only), 10% on unmixed cases
delivery Free within 2 miles for over £200, otherwise £10 per delivery within M25; £10 per case outside M25. G T
❂ *A tempting list full of unusual wines you really want to drink – and you can try them on the spot, in the friendly wine bar,
which serves tapas-style food. The staff are knowledgeable, and there's a waiting list for the popular tutored tastings.*

Halifax Wine Company

18 Prescott Street, Halifax, West Yorkshire HX1 2LG (01422) 256333 e-mail andy@halifaxwinecompany.com
website www.halifaxwinecompany.com hours Tues–Wed 9–5, Thur–Fri 9–6, Sat 9–5. Closed first week in January and
first week in August cards Access, Maestro, MasterCard, Visa discounts 8% on 12 bottles or more (can be unsplit
cases) for personal callers to the shop delivery Free to HX postcodes on orders over £85; rest of UK mainland – orders of
£125 or over: £5.95 for first 12 bottles, then £4.95 per subsequent case/part cases. Orders under £125: £9.95 for first
12 bottles, then £4.95 per subsequent case/part cases. M
❂ *Exciting, wide-ranging and award-winning list, at keen prices. Portugal (fantastic list of Madeiras), Spain and Italy are the
strong points but there is plenty from the New World, too.*

Handford Wines

105 Old Brompton Road, South Kensington, London SW7 3LE (020) 7589 6113 fax (020) 7581 2983
e-mail jack@handford.net website www.handford.net hours Mon–Sat 10–8.30, Sun 12–4
cards AmEx, MasterCard, Visa discounts 5% on mixed cases delivery £8.50 for orders under £150 within UK
en primeur Bordeaux, Burgundy, Rhône, Port. G M T
❂ *Delightful London shop, absolutely packed with the sort of wines I really want to drink.*

hangingditch wine merchants

Britannic Buildings, 42–44 Victoria Street, Manchester M3 1ST (0161) 832 8222

e-mail wine@hangingditch.com website www.hangingditch.com hours Mon–Wed 10–6, Thur–Sat 10–8, Sun 12–5 (Sep–Dec only) cards AmEx, MasterCard, Visa, all debit cards discounts 5% on 6–11 bottles, 10% on 12 bottles or more delivery free for cases with 10 miles; national deliveries: charged at cost (e.g. £10 per case). G M T

✪ *Primarily a wine merchant but also promotes the 'vinoteca' concept – wines by the glass available from a rotating selection or by the bottle for retail price plus a fixed £6 corkage. Food and wine matching and bespoke tasting events and gourmet dinners also on offer.*

Roger Harris Wines

mail order Loke Farm, Weston Longville, Norfolk NR9 5LG (01603) 880171 fax (01603) 880291

e-mail sales@rogerharriswines.co.uk website www.rogerharriswines.co.uk hours Mon–Fri 9–5 cards AmEx, MasterCard, Visa delivery UK mainland, £4 for 1st case, £2 every additional case minimum order 1 mixed case. M

✪ *Britain's acknowledged experts in Beaujolais also have a good range of whites from the neighbouring Mâconnais region.*

Harvey Nichols

109–125 Knightsbridge, London SW1X 7RJ (020) 7235 5000 hours Mon–Sat 10–8, Sun 12–6

• The Mailbox, 31–32 Wharfside Street, Birmingham B1 1RE (0121) 616 6000 hours Mon–Sat 10–7, Sun 11–5

• 30–34 St Andrew Square, Edinburgh EH2 2AD (0131) 524 8388 hours Mon–Wed 10–6, Thur 10–8, Fri, Sat 10–7, Sun 11–6

• 107–111 Briggate, Leeds LS1 6AZ (0113) 204 8888 hours Mon–Wed 10–6, Thur 10–8, Fri–Sat 10–7, Sun 11–5

• 21 New Cathedral Street, Manchester M1 1AD (0161) 828 8888 hours Mon–Wed, Fri 10–7, Thur 10–8, Sat 9–7, Sun 11–5

website www.harveynichols.com cards AmEx, Maestro, MasterCard, Visa. T

✪ *Sought-after producers and cult fine wines, especially from France, Italy and California.*

Haynes Hanson & Clark

Sheep Street, Stow-on-the-Wold, Gloucestershire GL54 1AA (01451) 870808 fax (01451) 870508 hours Mon–Fri 9–6, Sat 9–5.30

• 7 Elystan Street, London SW3 3NT (020) 7584 7927 fax (020) 7584 7967 hours Mon–Fri 9–7, Sat 9–4.30

e-mail stow@hhandc.co.uk or london@hhandc.co.uk website www.hhandc.co.uk cards Maestro, MasterCard, Switch, Visa discounts 10% unsplit case delivery Free for 1 case or more in central London and areas covered by Stow-on-the-

Wold van; elsewhere 1 case £15.30, 2–3 cases £9.55 per case, 4 or more cases £7.95 per case, free on orders over £650   en primeur Bordeaux, Burgundy.   M T

✪ *Known for its subtle, elegant wines: top-notch Burgundy is the main focus of the list, but other French regions are well represented, and there's interesting stuff from Spain, Italy, Australia and New Zealand.*

Hedley Wright

11 Twyford Centre, London Road, Bishop's Stortford, Hertfordshire CM23 3YT (01279) 465818   fax (01279) 465819
hours Mon–Wed 9–6, Thur–Fri 9–7, Sat 10–6
• Wyevale Garden Centre, Cambridge Road, Hitchin, Hertfordshire SG4 0JT (01462) 431110   fax (01462) 422983
hours Mon–Fri 11–7, Sat 10–6, Sun 11–5
e-mail sales@hedleywright.co.uk   website www.hedleywright.co.uk   cards AmEx, Maestro, MasterCard, Visa
delivery £5 per delivery, free for orders over £100   minimum order 1 mixed case
en primeur Bordeaux, Chile, Germany, Port.   C G M T

✪ *A good all-round list, especially strong in France, Italy, Spain and South Africa.*

Hicks & Don

17 Kingsmead Business Park, Shaftesbury Road, Gillingham, Dorset SP8 5FB (01747) 824292   fax (01747) 826963
e-mail mailbox@hicksanddon.co.uk   website www.hicksanddon.co.uk   hours Mon–Fri 9–5
cards Maestro, MasterCard, Visa   discounts Negotiable   delivery Free over £100, otherwise £6 per case in UK mainland
minimum order 1 case   en primeur Bordeaux, Burgundy, Chile, Italy, Port, Rhône.   C G M T

✪ *Subtle, well-made wines that go with food, particularly French wines. Still plenty of choice under £10.*

Jeroboams (incorporating Laytons)

head office 7–9 Elliot's Place, London N1 8HX (020) 7288 8888   fax (020) 7359 2616   hours Mon–Fri 9–5.30
shops 50–52 Elizabeth Street, London SW1W 9PB (020) 7730 8108
• 20 Davies Street, London W1K 3DT (020) 7499 1015 • 13 Elgin Crescent, London W11 2JA (020) 7229 0527
• 29 Heath Street, London NW3 6TR (020) 7435 6845 • 96 Holland Park Avenue, London W11 3RB (020) 7727 9359
• 6 Pont Street, London SW1X 9EL (020) 7235 1612 • 1 St John's Wood High Street, London NW8 7NG (020) 7722 4020
• 56 Walton Street, London SW3 1RB (020) 7589 2020
• Mr Christian's Delicatessen, 11 Elgin Crescent, London W11 2JA (020) 7229 0501
• Milroy's of Soho, 3 Greek Street, London W1D 4NX (020) 7437 2385 (whisky and wine)
e-mail sales@jeroboams.co.uk   website www.jeroboams.co.uk   hours shops Mon–Sat 9–7 (may vary)

cards AmEx, Maestro, MasterCard, Visa delivery Free for orders over £285, otherwise £17.25 en primeur Bordeaux, Burgundy, Rhône. C G M T

✪ *Wide-ranging list of affordable and enjoyable wines, especially good in France, Italy, Australia and New Zealand. Fine foods, especially cheeses and olive oils, are available in the Holland Park and Mr Christian's Delicatessen shops.*

S H Jones

27 High Street, Banbury, Oxfordshire OX16 5EW (01295) 251179 fax (01295) 272352 e-mail banbury@shjones.com
• 9 Market Square, Bicester, Oxfordshire OX26 6AA (01869) 322448 e-mail bicester@shjones.com
• The Cellar Shop, 2 Riverside, Tramway Road, Banbury, Oxfordshire OX16 5TU (01295) 672296 fax (01295) 259560
e-mail retail@shjones.com • 121 Regent Street, Leamington Spa, Warwickshire CV32 4NU (01926) 315609
e-mail leamington@shjones.com website www.shjones.com hours Please call each store for details cards Maestro,
MasterCard, Visa delivery Free for 12 bottles of wine/spirits or total value over £100 within 15-mile radius of shops,
otherwise £9.75 per case en primeur Bordeaux, Burgundy, Port. C G M T

✪ *Wide-ranging list with good Burgundies and Rhônes, clarets from £16 and plenty of tasty stuff from elsewhere.*

Justerini & Brooks

mail order 61 St James's Street, London SW1A 1LZ (020) 7484 6400 fax (020) 7484 6499
e-mail justorders@justerinis.com website www.justerinis.com hours Mon–Fri 9–5.30 cards Maestro, MasterCard, Visa
delivery Free for unmixed cases over £250, otherwise £15 + VAT in UK mainland minimum order 1 case
en primeur Alsace, Bordeaux, Burgundy, Italy, Loire, Rhône, Germany. C M T

✪ *Superb list of top-quality wines from Europe's classic regions, as well as some excellent New World choices.*

Laithwaites Wine

mail order New Aquitaine House, Exeter Way, Theale, Reading, Berkshire RG7 4PL order line 0845 194 7700
fax 0845 194 7766 e-mail orders@laithwaites.co.uk website www.laithwaites.co.uk hours Mon–Fri 8–9, Sat–Sun
9–6 cards AmEx, Diners, Maestro, MasterCard, Visa discounts On unmixed cases of 6 or 12 delivery £6.99 per
delivery address minimum order no minimum order but most offers available in 6 or 12 bottle cases (mixed and unmixed)
en primeur Australia, Bordeaux, Burgundy, Rhône, Rioja. C M T
• Flagship store: The Arch, 219–221 Stoney Street, London SE1 9AA (020) 7407 6378 fax (020) 7407 5411
e-mail thearch@laithwaiteswine.com hours Mon–Thur 10–7, Fri 10–10, Sat 10–8, Sun 12–6

✪ *Mail order specialist with new flagship store just off Borough Market and 10 other shops in the South-East and the Midlands. Extensive selection of wines from France, Australia, Spain, Italy and elsewhere.*

Lay & Wheeler

mail order Holton Park, Holton St Mary, Suffolk CO7 6NN 0845 330 1855   fax 0845 330 4095
e-mail sales@laywheeler.com   website www.laywheeler.com hours (Order office) Mon–Fri 8.30–5.30
cards Maestro, MasterCard, Visa   delivery £9.95; free for orders over £200
en primeur Bordeaux, Burgundy, Port (some vintages), Rhône, Spain.   C M T
✪ *A must-have list with first-class Bordeaux and Burgundy to satisfy the most demanding drinker, and plenty more besides. En primeur and fine wines are two core strengths here.*

Lea & Sandeman

170 Fulham Road, London SW10 9PR (020) 7244 0522   fax (020) 7244 0533
• 51 High Street, Barnes, London SW13 9LN (020) 8878 8643 • 211 Kensington Church Street, London W8 7LX
(020) 7221 1982 • 167 Chiswick High Road, London W4 2DR (020) 8995 7355   e-mail info@leaandsandeman.co.uk
website www.leaandsandeman.co.uk   hours Mon–Sat 10–8   cards AmEx, Maestro, MasterCard, Visa   discounts 5–15%
by case, other discounts on 10 cases or more   delivery London £10 for less than £100, otherwise free, and free to UK
mainland south of Perth on orders over £250, otherwise £15   en primeur Bordeaux, Burgundy, Italy.   C G M T
✪ *Burgundy and Italy take precedence here, and there's a succession of excellent names, chosen with great care by Charles Lea and Patrick Sandeman. Bordeaux has wines at all price levels, and there are short but fascinating ranges from the USA, Spain, Australia and New Zealand.*

Liberty Wines

mail order Unit D18, The Food Market, New Covent Garden, London SW8 5LL (020) 7720 5350   fax (020) 7720 6158
e-mail order@libertywines.co.uk   website www.libertywines.co.uk   hours Mon–Fri 9–5.30   cards Maestro, MasterCard,
Visa   delivery Free to mainland UK   minimum order 12 x 75cl bottles.   M
✪ *Italy rules, with superb wines from pretty well all the best producers. Liberty are the UK agents for most of their producers, so if you're interested in Italian wines this should be your first port of call. Also top names from Australia and elsewhere.*

Linlithgow Wines

Crossford, Station Road, Linlithgow, West Lothian EH49 6BW (01506) 848821   e-mail jrobmcd@aol.com
website www.linlithgowwines.co.uk   hours flexible (please phone first)   cards None: cash, cheque or bank transfer only
delivery Free locally; elsewhere in UK £9 for 1 case, £15 for 2 cases and £5 per case thereafter.   G M T
✪ *Terrific list of French wines, many imported direct from family-run vineyards in southern France.*

O W Loeb & Co

mail order 3 Archie Street, off Tanner Street, London SE1 3JT (020) 7234 0385 fax (020) 7357 0440
e-mail finewine@owloeb.com website www.owloeb.com hours Mon–Fri 8.30–5.30 cards Maestro, MasterCard, Visa
discounts 3 cases and above delivery Free 3 cases or more and on orders over £250 minimum order 1 case
en primeur Burgundy, Bordeaux, Rhône, Germany (Mosel). C M T
✪ *Burgundy, the Rhône, Loire and Germany stand out, with top producers galore. Then there are Loeb's new discoveries from Spain and the New World, especially New Zealand and South Africa.*

Maison du Vin

Moor Hill, Hawkhurst, Kent TN18 4PF (01580) 753487 fax (01580) 755627 e-mail kvgriffin@aol.com
website www.maison-du-vin.co.uk hours Mon 10–4, Tue–Fri 10–5, Sat 10–6 cards Access, AmEx, Maestro,
MasterCard, Visa delivery Free locally; UK mainland at cost en primeur Bordeaux. C G M T
✪ *As the name suggests, the focus is on French wines, and interesting wines, not brands. There is some good stuff from Australia and Chile – at prices from about £6 upwards. There's a monthly themed 'wine school' or you can book personal tutored tastings.*

Majestic (see also Wine and Beer World page 189)

head office Majestic House, Otterspool Way, Watford, Herts WD25 8WW (01923) 298200
fax (01923) 819105; 153 stores nationwide e-mail info@majestic.co.uk website www.majestic.co.uk
hours Mon–Fri 10–8, Sat 9–7, Sun 10–5 (may vary) cards AmEx, Diners, Maestro, MasterCard, Visa
delivery Free UK mainland minimum order 1 mixed case (6 bottles) en primeur Bordeaux, Port, Burgundy. G M T
✪ *One of the best places to buy Champagne, with a good range and good discounts for buying in quantity. Loads of interesting and reasonably priced stuff, especially from France, Germany and the New World.*

Marks & Spencer

head office Waterside House, 35 North Wharf Road, London W2 1NW (020) 7935 4422 fax (020) 7487 2679;
600 licensed stores website www.marksandspencer.com hours Variable discounts Variable, a selection of 10 different Wines of the Month, buy any 6 and save 10% in selected stores. M T
✪ *M&S works with top producers around the world to create its impressive list of own-label wines. All the wines are exclusive and unique to M&S, selected by their in-house winemaking team.*

The following services are available where indicated: C = cellarage **G** = glass hire/loan **M** = mail/online order **T** = tastings and talks

Martinez Wines

35 The Grove, Ilkley, Leeds, West Yorkshire LS29 9NJ (01943) 600000 fax 0870 922 3940 e-mail shop@martinez.co.uk
website www.martinez.co.uk hours Sun 12–6, Mon–Wed 10–8, Thur–Fri 10–9, Sat 9.30–6 cards AmEx, Maestro,
MasterCard, Visa discounts 5% on 6 bottles or more, 10% on orders over £150 delivery Free local delivery, otherwise
£13.99 per case mainland UK en primeur Bordeaux, Burgundy. C G M T
✪ *From a wide-ranging list, I'd single out the selections from France, Italy, Spain, Australia, Argentina and South Africa.*

Millésima

mail order 87 Quai de Paludate, CS 11691, 33050 Bordeaux Cedex, France (00 33) 5 57 80 88 08
fax (00 33) 5 57 80 88 19 Freephone 0800 917 0352 website www.millesima.com hours Mon–Fri 8–5.30
cards AmEx, Diners, Maestro, MasterCard, Visa delivery For bottled wines, free to single UK addresses for orders
exceeding £500. Otherwise, a charge of £20 will be applied. For en primeur wines, free to single UK addresses.
en primeur Bordeaux, Burgundy, Rhône. C M T
✪ *Wine comes direct from the châteaux to Millésima's 200-year-old cellars, where 2.5 million bottles are stored. Bordeaux
and Burgundy are the core strengths, with vintages going back to the 1980s and including a large selection of magnums,
double magnums, jeroboams (5 litres) and imperiales (6 litres). Plus a sprinkling of established names from Alsace, the
Rhône and Champagne.*

Montrachet

mail order 11 Catherine Place, London SW1E 6DX (020) 7821 1337 e-mail tim@montrachetwine.com
website www.montrachetwine.com hours Mon–Fri 8.30–5.30 cards Maestro, MasterCard, Visa
delivery England and Wales £15, free for 3 or more cases; for Scotland ring for details
minimum order 1 unmixed case en primeur Bordeaux, Burgundy. C M T
✪ *Impressive Burgundies are the main attraction here, but there are also some very good Rhônes, and Bordeaux is excellent
at all price levels.*

Moreno Wines

11 Marylands Road, London W9 2DU (020) 7286 0678 fax (020) 7286 0513 e-mail merchant@moreno-wines.co.uk
website www.morenowinedirect.com hours Mon–Fri 4–8, Sat 12–8 cards AmEx, Maestro, MasterCard, Visa
discounts 10% on 1 or more cases delivery Up to 1 case £8, up to 2 cases £10, free thereafter. M T
✪ *Specialist in Spanish wines, from everyday drinking to fine and rare wines from older vintages, with a few well-chosen
additions from Australia, Italy and elsewhere.*

Wm Morrisons Supermarkets

head office Hilmore House, Gain Lane, Bradford, West Yorkshire BD3 7DL 0845 611 5000 fax 0845 611 6801
371 licensed branches customer service 0845 611 6111; Mon–Fri 8–6.30, Sat 9–5 website www.morrisons.co.uk
hours Variable, generally Mon–Sat 8–8, Sun 10–4 cards AmEx, Delta, Maestro, MasterCard, Solo, Style, Visa Electron. G T
✪ *Inexpensive, often tasty wines, and if you're prepared to trade up a little there's some really good stuff here.*

New Zealand House of Wine

mail order/online based near Petworth, Surrey e-mail info@nzhouseofwine.com website www.nzhouseofwine.co.uk
order freephone 0800 085 6273 enquiries (01428) 70 77 33 fax (01428) 70 77 66 hours Mon–Fri, UK office hours
cards AmEx, Delta, Maestro, MasterCard, Visa, Visa Debit discounts often available on high-volume orders (60+ bottles)
for parties, weddings and other events delivery UK mainland only: free delivery for orders above £200, £5.99 for orders
above £100, £9.59 for orders less than £100. M
✪ *Impressive list of over 300 New Zealand wines, with plenty under £10 and some really fine stuff around £20 and over.*

James Nicholson

7/9 Killyleagh Street, Crossgar, Co. Down, Northern Ireland BT30 9DQ (028) 4483 0091 fax (028) 4483 0028
e-mail shop@jnwine.com website www.jnwine.com hours Mon–Sat 10–7 cards Maestro, MasterCard, Visa
discounts 10% mixed case delivery Free (1 case or more) in Eire and Northern Ireland; UK mainland £10.95,
2 cases £15.95 en primeur Bordeaux, Burgundy, California, Rioja, Rhône. C G M T
✪ *Well-chosen list mainly from small, committed growers around the world. Bordeaux, Rhône and southern France are
slightly ahead of the field, there's a good selection of Burgundy and some excellent drinking from Germany and Spain.*

Nickolls & Perks

37 Lower High Street, Stourbridge, West Midlands DY8 1TA (01384) 394518 fax (01384) 440786
e-mail sales@nickollsandperks.co.uk website www.nickollsandperks.co.uk hours Tues–Fri 10.30–5.30, Sat 10.30–5
cards Maestro, MasterCard, Visa discounts negotiable per case delivery £10 per consignment; free over £150
en primeur Bordeaux, Champagne, Port. C G M T
✪ *Established in 1797, Nickolls & Perks have a wide-ranging list – and a terrific website – covering most areas.
Their strength is France. Advice is available to clients wishing to develop their cellars or invest in wine.*

Nidderdale Fine Wines

2a High Street, Pateley Bridge, North Yorkshire HG3 5AW (01423) 711703 e-mail mike@southaustralianwines.com

website www.southaustralianwines.com hours Tues–Sat 10–6 cards Maestro, MasterCard, Visa
discounts 5% case discount on shop purchases for 12+ bottles delivery £5 per 12-bottle case in England, Wales and southern Scotland. Single bottle delivery available. G T
✪ *Specialist in South Australia, with 300 wines broken down into regions. Also 350 or so wines from the rest of the world. Look out for online offers and winemaker dinners.*

Noble Rot Wine Warehouses

18 Market Street, Bromsgrove, Worcestershire B61 8DA (01527) 575606 fax (01527) 833133
e-mail info@noble-rot.co.uk website www.noble-rot.co.uk hours Mon–Sat 9.30–5.30
cards Maestro, MasterCard, Visa discounts Various delivery Free within 10-mile radius. G T
✪ *Australia, Italy, France and Spain feature strongly in a frequently changing list of more than 400 wines, mostly at £5–15.*

O'Briens

head office 33 Spruce Avenue, Stillorgan Industrial Park, Co. Dublin, Ireland (low cost number) 1850 269 777
fax 01 269 7480; 28 stores e-mail sales@obrienswines.ie; info@obrienswines.ie website www.wine.ie
hours Mon–Sat 10.30am–10pm, Sun 1–10pm cards MasterCard, Visa delivery €10 per case anywhere in Ireland (minimum order 6 bottles); free for orders over €200 en primeur Bordeaux. G M T
✪ *Family-owned drinks retailer, which could well claim to be the best of the chains in Ireland. Imports directly from over 75 wineries worldwide.*

Oddbins

head office 31–33 Weir Road, London SW19 8UG (020) 8944 4400; 131 shops nationwide fax (020) 8944 4411
mail order Oddbins Direct 0800 328 2323 fax 0800 328 3848 website www.oddbins.com hours Vary
cards AmEx, Maestro, MasterCard, Visa, Visa Electron, Delta, Solo discounts 20% off any 12 bottles of wine or more
delivery Free locally for orders over £100 en primeur Bordeaux. G M T
✪ *Buzzing again under new ownership (one of the owners is Simon Baile, son of the original founder). A lot of dross has been cleared out and over 400 new wines added to the range – hand-picked wines from small growers, just like the old Oddbins of yore. You get a good discount if you buy a case (12 bottles).*

Old Chapel Cellars

The Old Chapel, Millpool, Truro, Cornwall TR1 1EX (01872) 270545 e-mail jamie@oldchapelcellars.co.uk
website www.oldchapelcellars.co.uk hours Mon–Sat 10–6 cards Maestro, MasterCard, Visa

delivery £7.99 per case UK mainland; free for orders over £95. G M T

✪ *Excellent, knowledgeable list that specializes in Spain and Portugal, plus wines from all over the world.*

The Oxford Wine Company

The Wine Warehouse, Witney Road, Standlake, Oxfordshire OX29 7PR (01865) 301144 fax (01865) 301155
e-mail orders@oxfordwine.co.uk website www.oxfordwine.co.uk hours Mon–Sat 9–7, Sun 11–4

• 165 Botley Road, Oxford OX2 0PB (01865) 249500 hours Mon–Sat 10–8, Sun 10–5

• Units 1 & 2, Baytree Court, The Chippings, Tetbury, Gloucestershire GL8 8EU hours Mon–Sat 9–6
cards AmEx, Diners, Maestro, MasterCard, Visa discounts 5% discount on a case of 12
delivery Free locally; national delivery £9.99 for any amount en primeur Bordeaux. G M T

✪ *A good selection from the classic regions and the New World, from bargain basement prices to expensive fine wines.*

OZ WINES

mail order Oz Wines, Freepost RSHB-HHTE-CZGH, Berkshire SL6 5AQ (0845) 4501261 e-mail sales@ozwines.co.uk
website www.ozwines.co.uk hours Mon–Fri 9.30–7 cards Almost all major credit cards delivery Free
minimum order 1 mixed case. M T

✪ *Australian wines made by small wineries and real people – with the thrilling flavours that Australians do better than anyone.*

Penistone Court Wine Cellars

The Railway Station, Penistone, Sheffield, South Yorkshire S36 6HP (01226) 766037 fax (01226) 767310
e-mail orders@pcwine.plus.com website www.pcwine.co.uk hours Tues–Fri 10–6, Sat 10–3 cards Maestro,
MasterCard, Visa delivery Free locally, rest of UK mainland charged at cost minimum order 1 mixed case. G M

✪ *A well-balanced list, with something from just about everywhere, mostly from familiar names.*

Philglas & Swiggot

21 Northcote Road, Battersea, London SW11 1NG (020) 7924 4494

• 64 Hill Rise, Richmond, London TW10 6UB (020) 8332 6031

• 22 New Quebec Street, Marylebone, London W1H 7SB (020) 7402 0002

e-mail info@philglas-swiggot.co.uk website www.philglas-swiggot.co.uk hours Mon–Sat 11–7, Sun 12–5
cards AmEx, Maestro, MasterCard, Visa discounts 5% per case delivery Free 1 case locally, or £5 elsewhere. G M

✪ *Excellent selections from Australia, Italy, France and Austria – subtle, interesting wines, rather than blockbuster brands. Subscriber's club with estate wines, bin ends and limited allocation wines.*

Christopher Piper Wines

1 Silver Street, Ottery St Mary, Devon EX11 1DB (01404) 814139 fax (01404) 812100
e-mail sales@christopherpiperwines.co.uk website www.christopherpiperwines.co.uk
hours Mon–Fri 8.30–5.30, Sat 9–4.30 cards Maestro, MasterCard, Visa discounts 5% mixed case, 10% 3 or more
cases delivery £8.95 for 1 case then £4.80 for each case, free for orders over £220 minimum order (for mail order)
1 mixed case en primeur Bordeaux, Burgundy, Rhône. C G M T
✪ *Huge range of well-chosen wines that reflect a sense of place and personality, with lots of information
to help you make up your mind.*

Terry Platt Wine Merchants

Council Street West, Llandudno LL30 1ED (01492) 874099 fax (01492) 874788 e-mail info@terryplattwines.co.uk
website www.terryplattwines.co.uk hours Mon–Fri 8.30–5.30 cards Access, Maestro, MasterCard, Visa
delivery Free locally and UK mainland 5 cases or more minimum order 1 mixed case. G M T
✪ *A wide-ranging list with a sprinkling of good growers from most regions.*

Playford Ros

Middle Park, Thirsk, Yorkshire YO7 3AH (01845) 522334 fax (01845) 526888 e-mail sales@playfordros.com
website www.playfordros.com hours Mon–Fri 8–5 cards MasterCard, Visa discounts Negotiable
delivery Free Yorkshire, Derbyshire, Durham, Newcastle; elsewhere £10–15 or at courier cost
minimum order 1 mixed case en primeur Bordeaux, Burgundy. G M T
✪ *A carefully chosen list, with reassuringly recognizable Burgundy, exceptional Australian and good stuff from other French
regions, Chile, Oregon and New Zealand. Plenty at the £6–8 mark.*

Portland Wine Company

152a Ashley Road, Hale, Altrincham, Cheshire WA15 9SA (0161) 928 0357 fax (0161) 905 1291
• 54 London Road, Alderley Edge, Cheshire SK5 7DX (01625) 590919
• 82 Chester Road, Macclesfield, Cheshire SK11 8DA (01625) 616147
• 45–47 Compstall Road, Marple Bridge, Cheshire SK6 5HG (0161) 426 0155
• 44 High Street, Tarporley, Cheshire CW6 0DX (01829) 730 762
e-mail info@portlandwine.co.uk website www.portlandwine.co.uk hours Mon–Fri 10–9, Sat 9–9

The following services are available where indicated: C = cellarage **G** = glass hire/loan **M** = mail/online order **T** = tastings and talks

cards Maestro, MasterCard, Visa discounts 5% on 2 cases or more, 10% on 5 cases or more delivery Free locally,
£15 + VAT per consignment nationwide, no minimum order en primeur Bordeaux. C T
✪ *Spain, Portugal and Burgundy are specialities and there's a promising-looking list of clarets. Consumer-friendly list with
something at every price level from around the world.*

Private Cellar
mail order 51 High Street, Wicken, Cambridgeshire CB7 5XR (01353) 721999 fax (01353) 724074
e-mail orders@privatecellar.co.uk website www.privatecellar.co.uk hours Mon–Fri 8–6 cards Delta, Maestro,
MasterCard, Visa delivery £14.50, or free for orders of 24+ bottles in mainland England and Wales. For Scotland, islands,
Northern Ireland and worldwide, phone for quote en primeur Bordeaux, Burgundy, Rhône, Germany, Port, California. C M T
✪ *Friendly, personal wine advice is part of the service; wines are predominantly French, with lots of 'everyday claret'
at £10–15.*

Quaff Fine Wine Merchant
139–141 Portland Road, Hove BN3 5QJ (01273) 820320 fax (01273) 820326 e-mail sales@quaffit.com
website www.quaffit.com hours Mon–Thur 10.30–7.30, Fri–Sat 10–8, Sun 12–7
cards Access, Maestro, MasterCard, Visa discounts 10% mixed case delivery Next working day nationwide,
charge depends on order value. C G M T
✪ *Extensive and keenly priced list organized by grape variety rather than by country.*

Raeburn Fine Wines
21–23 Comely Bank Road, Edinburgh EH4 1DS (0131) 343 1159 fax (0131) 332 5166
e-mail sales@raeburnfinewines.com website www.raeburnfinewines.com hours Mon–Sat 9.30–6
cards AmEx, Maestro, MasterCard, Visa discounts 5% unsplit case, 2.5% mixed case delivery Free local area 1 or more
cases (usually); elsewhere at cost en primeur Australia, Bordeaux, Burgundy, California, Germany, Italy, Languedoc-
Roussillon, Loire, New Zealand, Rhône. G M T
✪ *Carefully chosen list, mainly from small growers. Italy and France – especially Burgundy – are specialities,
with Germany, Austria and northern Spain close behind, as well as selected Port and sought-after California wines such as
Shafer Vineyards and Turley Cellars.*

The Real Wine Company
mail order c/o Pinewood Nurseries, Wexham Street, Stoke Poges, Buckinghamshire SL3 6NB (01753) 664190

e-mail mark@therealwineco.co.uk website www.therealwineco.co.uk cards Delta, Maestro, MasterCard, Visa, AmEx delivery £6.99 per order, orders over £250 free minimum order 1 mixed case.

✪ *Owner Mark Hughes has based his list entirely on his personal taste – check it out and see if you agree with his lively tasting notes. There are plenty of good-value wines.There are also wine and food matches, with recipe suggestions. Under the same ownership as the Chilean Wine Club (see page 163).*

Reid Wines

The Mill, Marsh Lane, Hallatrow, Nr Bristol BS39 6EB (01761) 452645 fax (01761) 453642 e-mail reidwines@aol.com hours Mon–Fri 9–5.30 cards Access, Maestro, MasterCard, Visa (3% charge) delivery Free within 25 miles of Hallatrow (Bristol), and in central London for orders over 2 cases en primeur Claret. C G M T

✪ *A mix of great old wines, some old duds and splendid current stuff. Italy, USA, Australia, port and Madeira look tremendous.*

Reserve Wines

176 Burton Road, West Didsbury, Manchester M20 1LH (0161) 438 0101 e-mail sales@reservewines.co.uk website www.reservewines.co.uk hours Mon–Fri 12–9, Sat 11–9, Sun 12–7 cards Delta, Maestro, MasterCard, Solo, Switch, Visa delivery Starts from £8.

✪ *Award-winning wine specialist established in 2003 and focusing on making the world of wine accessible and fun.*

Howard Ripley

mail order 25 Dingwall Road, London SW18 3AZ (020) 8877 3065 fax (020) 8877 0029 e-mail info@howardripley.com website www.howardripley.com hours Mon–Fri 9–6 cards Maestro, MasterCard, Visa delivery Minimum charge £11.50 + VAT, free UK mainland on orders over £600 ex-VAT en primeur Burgundy, Germany, Oregon, New Zealand, Switzerland. C M T

✪ *A must-have list for serious Burgundy lovers; expensive but not excessive, and including a great backlist of older vintages. The German range is also excellent.*

Roberson

348 Kensington High Street, London W14 8NS (020) 7371 2121 fax (020) 7371 4010 e-mail enquiries@roberson.co.uk website www.robersonwinemerchant.co.uk; www.roberson.co.uk hours Mon–Sat 10–8, Sun 12–6 cards Access, AmEx, Maestro, MasterCard, Visa discounts (mail order) 5% on Champagne and spirits, 10% on wine cases delivery Free delivery within London, otherwise £15 per case en primeur Bordeaux, Port. C G M T

✪ *Fine and rare wines, sold by the bottle. All of France is excellent; so is Italy and port. With friendly, knowledgeable staff, the shop is well worth a visit.*

The RSJ Wine Company

33 Coin Street, London SE1 9NR (020) 7928 4554 fax (020) 7928 9768 e-mail tom.king@rsj.uk.com
website www.rsj.uk.com hours Mon–Fri 9–6, answering machine at other times
cards AmEx, Maestro, MasterCard, Visa delivery Free central London, minimum 1 case; England and Wales (per case), £14.10 1 case, £10.25 2 cases or more. G M T
✪ *A roll-call of great Loire names, and some good Bordeaux.*

Sainsbury's

head office 33 Holborn, London EC1N 2HT (020) 7695 6000 customer service 0800 636262; 876 stores
website www.sainsburys.co.uk online groceries helpline 0800 328 1700 hours Variable, some 24 hrs, locals Mon–Sat 7–11, Sun 10 or 11–4 cards AmEx, Maestro, MasterCard, Visa discounts 5% for 6 bottles or more. G M T
✪ *A collection to cater for bargain hunters as well as lovers of good-value wine higher up the scale. They've expanded their Taste the Difference range and got some top producers on board.*

The Sampler

266 Upper Street, London N1 2UQ (020) 7226 9500 fax (020) 7226 6555 e-mail jamie@thesampler.co.uk
website www.thesampler.co.uk hours Mon–Sat 11.30–9
• 35 Thurloe Place, London SW7 2HJ hours Mon–Sat 11.30–9, Sun 11.30–7
cards Maestro, MasterCard, Visa delivery Free locally for minimum 1 case; £10 elsewhere on UK mainland. Next day and Sat deliveries at extra cost discounts 10% for 6 bottles or more, or to online orders over £75. G M T
✪ *The future of wine retailing? 1200 wines in the range (strengths include older vintages of Bordeaux and Rioja, sherry and grower Champagnes), long opening hours, email newsletters and Enomatic sampling machines allowing you to taste up to 80 wines before buying. Regular tastings and courses.*

Savage Selection

The Ox House, Market Place, Northleach, Cheltenham, Glos GL54 3EG (01451) 860896 fax (01451) 860996
• The Ox House Shop and Wine Bar at same address (01451) 860680 e-mail wine@savageselection.co.uk
website www.savageselection.co.uk hours Office Mon–Fri 9–6; shop and wine bar Tue–Sat 10–10 cards Maestro, MasterCard, Visa delivery Free locally for orders over £100; elsewhere on UK mainland free for orders over £250;

smaller orders £10 + VAT for 1 case and £5 + VAT for each additional case en primeur Bordeaux. C G M T

✪ *Owner Mark Savage MW seeks out wines of genuine originality and personality from small family estates. France is the mainstay, alongside wines from Slovenia, Austria, Oregon and elsewhere.*

Seckford Wines

Dock Lane, Melton, Suffolk IP12 1PE (01394) 446622 fax (01394) 446633 e-mail sales@seckfordwines.co.uk
website www.seckfordwines.co.uk cards Maestro, MasterCard, Visa delivery £14.10 per consignment in UK mainland; elsewhere at cost minimum order 1 mixed case en primeur Bordeaux, Burgundy. C M

✪ *Bordeaux, Burgundy, Champagne and the Rhône are the stars of this list, with some excellent older vintages. Serious stuff from Italy and Spain, too.*

Selfridges

400 Oxford Street, London W1A 1AB 0800 123 400 (for all stores) hours London Mon–Sat 9.30–9, Sun 12–6
• Upper Mall East, Bullring, Birmingham B5 4BP Mon–Fri 10–8 (Thur 10–9), Sat 9–8, Sun 11–5
• 1 Exchange Square, Manchester M3 1BD • The Trafford Centre, Manchester M17 8DA hours both Manchester branches Mon–Fri 10–8 (Thur 10–9), Sat 9–8, Sun 11–5
e-mail wineshop@selfridges.co.uk website www.selfridges.com cards AmEx, Maestro, MasterCard, Visa
discounts 10% case discount delivery £10 within 3 working days, UK mainland. T

✪ *Strong fine wine list with a wide range of classic wines, from Bordeaux through to Tokaji from Hungary. Great selection for gifts – as well as less expensive bottles, there are plenty of highly sought-after wines at £500-plus and you can even buy a bottle of Screaming Eagle, one of Napa's hottest properties, for £2400. Regular tastings.*

Somerfield See Co-operative Group

Sommelier Wine Co

23 St George's Esplanade, St Peter Port, Guernsey, Channel Islands GY1 2BG (01481) 721677 fax (01481) 716818
hours Mon–Sat 9.15–5.30, except Fri 9.15–6 cards Maestro, MasterCard, Visa discounts 5% 1 case or more
delivery Free locally (minimum 1 mixed case); being outside the European Community and with Customs restrictions means that the shipping of wine to the UK mainland is not possible. G T

✪ *An excellent list, with interesting, unusual wines.*

The following services are available where indicated: C = cellarage G = glass hire/loan M = mail/online order T = tastings and talks

Stainton Wines

1 Station Yard, Station Road, Kendal, Cumbria LA9 6BT (01539) 731886   fax (01539) 730396
e-mail admin@stainton-wines.co.uk   website www.stainton-wines.co.uk   hours Mon–Fri 9–5.30, Sat 9–4.30
cards Maestro, MasterCard, Visa   discounts 5% mixed case   delivery Free Cumbria and North Lancashire;
elsewhere (per case) £13 1 case, more than 1 case variable. G M T
✪ *The list includes some great Bordeaux, interesting Burgundy, and leading names from Italy and Chile.*

Stevens Garnier

47 West Way, Botley, Oxford OX2 OJF (01865) 263303   fax (01865) 791594   e-mail shop@stevensgarnier.co.uk
website www.stevensgarnier.co.uk   hours Mon–Thur 10–6, Fri 10–7, Sat 10–5   cards AmEx, Maestro, MasterCard, Visa,
Solo   discounts 10% on 12 bottles   delivery Free locally. G M T
✪ *Regional France is a strength: this is one of the few places in the UK you can buy wine from Savoie. Likewise,
there are interesting choices from Portugal, Australia, Chile and Canada.*

Stone, Vine & Sun

mail order No. 13 Humphrey Farms, Hazeley Road, Twyford, Winchester, Hampshire SO21 1QA (01962) 712351
fax (01962) 717545   e-mail sales@stonevine.co.uk   website www.stonevine.co.uk   hours Mon–Fri 9–6, Sat 9.30–4
cards Access, Maestro, MasterCard, Visa   discounts 5% on an unmixed case   delivery £5.50 for 1st case, £8.50 for
2 cases, free for orders over £250. Prices vary for Scottish Highlands, islands and Northern Ireland. G M T
✪ *Lovely list marked by enthusiasm and passion for the subject. Lots of interesting stuff from France, especially the Rhône,
Burgundy, Languedoc-Roussillon and the Loire. South Africa and South America are other strong areas, plus there are wines
from Germany, New Zealand, the USA and elsewhere.*

Sunday Times Wine Club

mail order New Aquitaine House, Exeter Way, Theale, Reading, Berkshire RG7 4PL   order line 0870 220 0020
fax 0870 220 0030   e-mail orders@sundaytimeswineclub.co.uk   website www.sundaytimeswineclub.co.uk
hours Mon–Fri 8–11, Sat–Sun 8–9   cards AmEx, Diners, Maestro, MasterCard, Visa   delivery £5.99 per order
en primeur Australia, Bordeaux, Burgundy, Rhône. C M T
✪ *Essentially the same as Laithwaites (see page 172), though the special offers come round at different times.
The membership fee is £10 per annum. The club runs tours and tasting events for its members.*

The following services are available where indicated: C = cellarage **G** = glass hire/loan **M** = mail/online order **T** = tastings and talks

Swig

mail order/online 188 Sutton Court Road, London W4 3HR (020) 8995 7060 or freephone 08000 272 272
fax (020) 8995 6195 e-mail wine@swig.co.uk website www.swig.co.uk cards Amex, MasterCard, Switch, Visa
minimum order 12 bottles delivery £9.50 per address en primeur Bordeaux, Burgundy, South Africa. C G M T
✪ *Seriously good wines sold in an unserious way. For instant recommendations there's a list of 'current favourites'*
organized in price bands; there's lots between £8 and £20 and the list covers pretty much everything you might want.

T & W Wines

5 Station Way, Brandon, Suffolk IP27 0BH (01842) 814414 fax (01842) 819967 e-mail contact@tw-wines.com
website www.tw-wines.com hours Mon–Fri 9–5.30, occasional Sat 9.30–1 cards AmEx, MasterCard, Visa
delivery (Most areas) 7–23 bottles £18.95 + VAT, 2 or more cases free en primeur Burgundy. C G M T
✪ *A good list, particularly if you're looking for interesting wines from Burgundy, Rhône, Alsace or the Loire, but prices are*
not especially low.

Tanners

26 Wyle Cop, Shrewsbury, Shropshire SY1 1XD (01743) 234500 fax (01743) 234501 hours Mon–Sat 9–6
• 36 High Street, Bridgnorth WV16 4DB (01746) 763148 fax (01746) 769798 hours Mon–Sat 9–5.30
• 4 St Peter's Square, Hereford HR1 2PG (01432) 272044 fax (01432) 263316 hours Mon–Sat 9–5.30
• Council Street West, Llandudno LL30 1ED (01492) 874099 fax (01492) 874788 hours Mon–Fri 9–5.30
• Severn Farm Enterprise Park, Welshpool SY21 7DF (01938) 552542 fax (01938) 556565 hours Mon–Fri 9–5.30,
Sat 9–1
e-mail sales@tanners-wines.co.uk website www.tanners-wines.co.uk cards Maestro, MasterCard, Visa
discounts 5% 1 mixed case, 7.5% 3 mixed cases (cash & collection); 5% for 3 mixed cases, 7.5% for 5 (mail order)
delivery Free on orders over £90 to one address, otherwise £7.95 minimum order £25
en primeur Bordeaux, Burgundy, Rhône, Germany, Port, occasionally others. C G M T
✪ *Outstanding, award-winning merchant: Bordeaux, Burgundy and Germany are terrific.*

Terroir Languedoc Wines

mail order/online Treetops, Grassington Road, Skipton, North Yorkshire BD23 1LL (01756) 700512 fax (01756) 797856
e-mail enquiries@terroirlanguedoc.co.uk website www.terroirlanguedoc.co.uk hours Mon–Fri 8–5 cards Maestro,
MasterCard, Visa discount Mixed case offers available alongside bespoke service. G M T
✪ *Hand-picked list of wines from interesting growers in one of France's most innovative regions.*

Tesco

head office Tesco House, PO Box 18, Delamare Road, Cheshunt EN8 9SL (01992) 632222 fax (01992) 630794
customer service 0800 505555; 1830 licensed branches e-mail customer.services@tesco.co.uk
website www.tesco.com hours Variable cards Maestro, MasterCard, Visa discounts 5% on 6 bottles or more. G M T
• online www.tesco.com discounts All cases include a 5% discount to match offers in-store, discounts vary monthly on
featured cases cards AmEx, Mastercard, Visa, Maestro, Clubcard Plus minimum order 1 case (12 bottles), 6 bottles for
Champagne delivery Choice of next day delivery or convenient 2-hour slots
✪ *A range of 850 wines from everyday drinking to fine wines. Tesco.com has an even greater selection by the case – over
1200 wines and champagnes. New features include a fine wine page and a next day delivery system.*

Turville Valley Wines

The Firs, Potter Row, Great Missenden, Bucks HP16 9LT (01494) 868818 fax (01494) 868832
e-mail chris@turville-valley-wines.com website www.turville-valley-wines.com
hours Mon–Fri 9–5.30 cards None delivery By arrangement minimum order £300 excluding VAT/12 bottles. C M
✪ *Top-quality fine and rare wines at trade prices.*

Valvona & Crolla

19 Elm Row, Edinburgh EH7 4AA (0131) 556 6066 fax (0131) 556 1668
e-mail wine@valvonacrolla.co.uk website www.valvonacrolla.co.uk
hours Shop: Mon–Sat 8.30–6, Sun 10.30–4, Caffe bar: Mon–Sat 8.30–5.30, Sun 10.30–3.30 cards AmEx, Maestro,
MasterCard, Visa discounts 7% 1–3 cases/24 bottles, 10% 4 or more cases delivery Free on orders over £150,
otherwise £10; Sat mornings free on orders over £200, otherwise £30. M T
✪ *Exciting selection of wines from all over the world, but specializing in Italy, including good selections from Abruzzo, Puglia,
Sicily and Sardinia, and 15 different Italian liqueurs.*

Villeneuve Wines

1 Venlaw Court, Peebles EH45 8AE (01721) 722500 fax (01721) 729922
• 82 High Street, Haddington EH41 3ET (01620) 822224 • 49A Broughton Street, Edinburgh EH1 3RJ (0131) 558 8441
e-mail wines@villeneuvewines.com website www.villeneuvewines.com hours (Peebles) Mon–Sat 10–8, Sun 12–5.30;
(Haddington) Mon–Sat 10–7; (Edinburgh) Mon–Wed 12–10, Thur–Sat 10–10, Sun 12–10
cards AmEx, Maestro, MasterCard, Visa delivery Free locally, £8.50 per case elsewhere. G M T
✪ *Italy, Australia and New Zealand are all marvellous here. France is good and Spain is clearly an enthusiasm, too.*

Vin du Van

mail order Colthups, The Street, Appledore, Kent TN26 2BX (01233) 758727 fax (01233) 758389
website www.vinduvan.co.uk hours Mon–Fri 9–5 cards Delta, Maestro, MasterCard, Visa
delivery Free locally; elsewhere £7.95 for 1st case, further cases free. For Highlands and islands, ask for quote
minimum order 1 mixed case. M
✪ *Extensive, wonderfully quirky, star-studded Australian list, one of the best in the UK; the kind of inspired lunacy I'd take to read on a desert island.*

Vinceremos

mail order Royal House, Sovereign Street, Leeds LS1 4BJ (0800) 107 3086 fax (0113) 288 4566
e-mail info@vinceremos.co.uk website www.vinceremos.co.uk hours Mon–Fri 8.30–5.30
cards AmEx, Delta, Maestro, MasterCard, Visa discounts 5% on 5 cases or more, 10% on 10 cases or more
delivery Free 5 cases or more. M
✪ *Organic specialist, with a wide-ranging list of wines, including biodynamic and Fairtrade. In addition to wine, you can buy fruit wine, beer, cider and perry, spirits, liqueurs and olive oil.*

Vintage Roots

mail order Holdshott Farm, Reading Road, Heckfield, Hook, Hampshire RG27 0JZ (0118) 932 6566, (0800) 980 4992
fax (0118) 922 5115 hours Mon–Fri 8.30–5.30, Sat in December e-mail info@vintageroots.co.uk
website www.vintageroots.co.uk cards Delta, Maestro, MasterCard, Visa discounts 5% on 5 cases or over
delivery £6.95 for any delivery under 5 cases; more than 6 cases is free. Some local deliveries free. Cases can be mixed. G M T
✪ *Everything on this list of over 300 wines is certified organic and/or biodynamic. As well as wine, Vintage Roots sell organic beer, cider, liqueurs, spirits and chocolate at Christmas time.*

Virgin Wines

mail order/online The Loft, St James' Mill, Whitefriars, Norwich NR3 1TN 0843 224 1001 fax (01603) 619277
e-mail help@virginwines.co.uk website www.virginwines.co.uk hours (Office) Mon–Fri 8–8, Sat–Sun 9–6
cards AmEx, Maestro, MasterCard, Visa, Paypal delivery £6.99 per order for all UK deliveries
minimum order 1 case. M T
✪ *Online retailer celebrating its first decade in 2010, with reasonably priced wines from all over the world. Additional features include a Wine Bank to help you save for your next case and online auctions.*

Waitrose

head office Doncastle Road, Southern Industrial Area, Bracknell, Berkshire RG12 8YA customer service 0800 188884, 228 licensed stores e-mail customer_service@waitrose.co.uk website www.waitrosewine.com
hours Mon–Sat 8.30–7, 8 or 9, Sun 10–4 or 11–5 cards AmEx, Delta, Maestro, MasterCard, Partnership Card, Visa
discounts Regular monthly promotions, 5% off for 6 bottles or more home delivery Available through www.waitrosedeliver.com and www.ocado.com and Waitrose Wine Direct (*below*)
en primeur Bordeaux and Burgundy available through Waitrose Wine Direct. G M T
• waitrose wine direct order online at www.waitrosewine.com or 0800 188881
e-mail wineadvisor@johnlewis.com discounts Vary monthly on featured cases; branch promotions are matched. All cases include a 5% discount to match branch offer. delivery Free standard delivery throughout UK mainland, Northern Ireland and Isle of Wight. Named day delivery, £6.95 per addressee (order by 6pm for next day – not Sun); next-day delivery before 10.30am, £9.95 per addressee (order by 6pm for next working day).
✪ *Ahead of the other supermarkets in quality, value and imagination. Still lots of tasty stuff under £5.*

Waterloo Wine Co

office and warehouse 6 Vine Yard, London SE1 1QL shop 59–61 Lant Street, London SE1 1QN (020) 7403 7967
fax (020) 7357 6976 e-mail sales@waterloowine.co.uk website www.waterloowine.co.uk
hours Mon–Fri 11–7.30, Sat 10–5 cards AmEx, Maestro, MasterCard, Visa delivery Free 1 case central London; elsewhere, 1 case £12, 2 cases £7.50 each. G T
✪ *Quirky, personal list, strong in the Loire and New Zealand.*

Wimbledon Wine Cellar

1 Gladstone Road, Wimbledon, London SW19 1QU (020) 8540 9979 fax (020) 8540 9399
e-mail enquiries@wimbledonwinecellar.com hours Mon–Sat 10–9
• 84 Chiswick High Road, London W4 1SY (020) 8994 7989 fax (020) 8994 3683
e-mail chiswick@wimbledonwinecellar.com hours Mon–Sat 10–9
• 4 The Boulevard, Imperial Wharf, Chelsea, London SW6 2UB (020) 7736 2191
e-mail chelsea@wimbledonwinecellar.com hours Mon–Sat 10–9, Sun 11–7
website www.wimbledonwinecellar.com cards AmEx, Maestro, MasterCard, Visa discounts 10% off 1 case (with a few exceptions), 20% off case of 6 Champagne delivery Free local delivery. Courier charges elsewhere
en primeur Burgundy, Bordeaux, Tuscany, Rhône. C G M T
✪ *Top names from Italy, Burgundy, Bordeaux, Rhône, Loire – and some of the best of the New World.*

Wine & Beer World (Majestic)

head office Majestic House, Otterspool Way, Watford, Hertfordshire WD25 8WW (01923) 298200
e-mail info@wineandbeer.co.uk website www.majesticinfrance.co.uk
• Rue du Judée, Zone Marcel Doret, Calais 62100, France (00 33) 3 21 97 63 00 e-mail calais@majestic.co.uk
hours 7 days 8–8, including Bank Holidays
• Centre Commercial Carrefour, Quai L'Entrepôt, Cherbourg 50100, France (00 33) 2 33 22 23 22
e-mail cherbourg@majestic.co.uk hours Mon–Sat 9–7
• Unit 3A, Zone La Française, Coquelles 62331, France (00 33) 3 21 82 93 64 e-mail coquelles@majestic.co.uk
hours 7 days 9–7, including Bank Holidays
pre-order (01923) 298297 discounts Available for large pre-orders cards Maestro, MasterCard, Visa. T
✪ The French arm of Majestic, with 300 wines at £2 less per bottle than UK prices. Calais is the largest branch and Coquelles the nearest to the Channel Tunnel terminal. English-speaking staff.

The Wine Company

mail order Town Barton, Doddiscombsleigh, Nr Exeter, Devon EX6 7PT (01647) 252005 e-mail nick@thewinecompany.biz
website www.thewinecompany.biz hours Mon–Sun 9–6 cards Maestro, MasterCard, Visa delivery £7.99 per case, free for orders over £150, UK mainland only. M
✪ The list of around 250 wines specializes in Australia and South Africa, with some top names you won't find anywhere else.

Wine Rack

head office Venus House, Brantwood Road, London N17 0YD (020) 8801 0011 fax (020) 8801 6455
e-mail info@winerack.co.uk website www.winerack.co.uk; 19 Wine Rack stores and more to come
hours Mon–Sat 10–10, Sun 11–10 cards Maestro, MasterCard, Visa delivery Free locally, some branches. G T
✪ Following the collapse in 2009 of First Quench (aka Thresher's and Wine Rack) a new owner has bought and revitalized a selection of Wine Rack stores in London and the Home Counties.

The Wine Society

mail order/online Gunnels Wood Road, Stevenage, Herts SG1 2BG (01438) 741177 fax (01438) 761167
order line (01438) 740222 e-mail memberservices@thewinesociety.com website www.thewinesociety.com
hours Mon–Fri 8.30–9, Sat 9–5; showroom: Mon–Fri 10–6, Thur 10–7, Sat 9.30–5.30
cards Delta, Maestro, MasterCard, Visa discounts (per case) £3 for pre-ordered collection delivery Free 1 case or more anywhere in UK; also collection facility at Templepatrick, County Antrim, and showroom and collection facility at Montreuil,

France, at French rates of duty and VAT en primeur Bordeaux, Burgundy, Germany, Port, Rhône. C G M T

✪ *An outstanding list from an inspired wine-buying team. Masses of well-chosen affordable wines as well as big names. The Wine Society regularly wins the UK's top awards for wine by mail order. Founded in 1874, The Wine Society's aim was, and remains, to introduce members to the best of the world's vineyards at a fair price. Holding a share in The Wine Society gives you a lifetime membership with no annual fee and no pressure to buy. The cost of a share is £40.*

The Wine Treasury

mail order 69–71 Bondway, London SW8 1SQ (020) 7793 9999

fax (020) 7793 8080 e-mail bottled@winetreasury.com website www.winetreasury.com hours Mon–Fri 9.30–6 cards Maestro, MasterCard, Visa discounts 10% for unmixed dozens delivery Free for orders over £200, England and Wales; Scotland phone for more details minimum order 1 mixed case. M

✪ *Excellent choices and top names from California and Italy – but they don't come cheap.*

Winemark the Wine Merchants

3 Duncrue Place, Belfast BT3 9BU (028) 9074 6274 fax (028) 9074 8022; 77 branches e-mail info@winemark.com website www.winemark.com hours Branches vary, but in general Mon–Sat 10–10, Sun 12–8 cards Switch, MasterCard, Visa discounts 5% on 6–11 bottles, 10% on 12 bottles or more. G M T

✪ *Over 500 wines, with some interesting wines from Australia, New Zealand, Chile and California.*

The Winery

4 Clifton Road, London W9 1SS (020) 7286 6475 fax (020) 7286 2733 e-mail info@thewineryuk.com website www.thewineryuk.com hours Mon–Sat 11–9.30, Sun and public holidays 12–8 cards Maestro, MasterCard, Visa discounts 5% on a mixed case delivery Free locally or for 3 cases or more, otherwise £10 per case. G M T

✪ *Largest selection of dry German wines in the UK. Burgundy, Rhône, Champagne, Italy and California are other specialities.*

WoodWinters

16 Henderson Street, Bridge of Allan, Scotland FK9 4HP (01786) 834894

• 91 Newington Road, Edinburgh EH9 1QW (0131) 667 2760

e-mail shop@woodwinters.com website www.woodwinters.com hours Mon–Sat 10–7; Sun 1–5 cards MasterCard, Switch, Visa discounts Vintners Dozen: buy 12 items or more and get a 13th free – we are happy to choose something appropriate for you delivery £8.95 per address; free for orders over £150 UK mainland. Islands and Northern Ireland, phone for quote en primeur Bordeaux, Burgundy, Italy, Rhone. C G M T

✪ *A young, ambitious operation, very strong on California and Australia, but also good stuff from Austria, Portugal, Italy, Spain and Burgundy. They do like flavour, so expect most of their wines to be mouth-filling. Wine tasting club and courses.*

Wright Wine Co

The Old Smithy, Raikes Road, Skipton, North Yorkshire BD23 1NP (0800) 328 4435 fax (01756) 798580
e-mail enquiries@wineandwhisky.co.uk website www.wineandwhisky.co.uk hours Mon–Fri 9–6; Sat 10–5:30; open
Sundays in December 10.30–4 cards Maestro, MasterCard, Visa discounts 10% unsplit case, 5% mixed case
delivery Free within 30 miles, elsewhere at cost. G
✪ *Equally good in both Old World and New World, with plenty of good stuff at keen prices. Wide choice of half bottles.*

Peter Wylie Fine Wines

Plymtree Manor, Plymtree, Cullompton, Devon EX15 2LE (01884) 277555 fax (01884) 277557
e-mail peter@wyliefinewines.co.uk website www.wyliefinewines.co.uk hours Mon–Fri 9–5.30
discounts Only on unsplit cases delivery Up to 3 cases in London £26, otherwise by arrangement. C M
✪ *Fascinating list of mature wines: Bordeaux from throughout the 20th century, vintage ports going back to the 1920s.*

Yapp Brothers

shop The Old Brewery, Water Street, Mere, Wiltshire BA12 6DY (01747) 860423 fax (01747) 860929
e-mail sales@yapp.co.uk website www.yapp.co.uk hours Mon–Sat 9–6 cards Maestro, MasterCard, Visa
discounts £6 per case on collection delivery £8 one case, 2 or more cases free. C G M T
✪ *Rhône and Loire specialists. Also some of the hard-to-find wines of Provence, Savoie, South-West France and Corsica, plus a small selection from Australia.*

Noel Young Wines

56 High Street, Trumpington, Cambridge CB2 9LS (01223) 566744 fax (01223) 844736
e-mail admin@nywines.co.uk website www.nywines.co.uk hours Mon–Fri 10–8, Sat 10–7, Sun 12–2
cards AmEx, Maestro, MasterCard, Visa discounts 5% for orders over £500 delivery Free over 12 bottles unless
discounted en primeur Australia, Burgundy, Italy, Rhône. G M T
✪ *Fantastic wines from just about everywhere. Australia is a particular passion and there is a great Austrian list, some terrific Germans, plus beautiful Burgundies, Italians and dessert wines.*

The following services are available where indicated: C = cellarage G = glass hire/loan M = mail/online order T = tastings and talks

Who's where

COUNTRYWIDE/MAIL ORDER/ONLINE
Adnams
Aldi
ASDA
AustralianWineCentre
Bancroft Wines
Bibendum Wine
Big Red Wine Co
Bordeaux Index
Anthony Byrne
ChateauOnline
Chilean Wine Club
Cockburns of Leith
Co-op
Croque-en-Bouche
Devigne Wines
Nick Dobson Wines
Domaine Direct
The Flying Corkscrew
FromVineyardsDirect
Roger Harris Wines
Jeroboams
Justerini & Brooks
Laithwaites
Lay & Wheeler
Laytons
Liberty Wines
O W Loeb
Majestic
Marks & Spencer
Millésima
Montrachet
Morrisons
New Zealand House of Wine
Oddbins
OZ WINES

Private Cellar
Real Wine Co
Howard Ripley
Sainsbury's
Stone, Vine & Sun
Sunday Times Wine Club
Swig
Tesco
Vin du Van
Vinceremos
Vintage Roots
Virgin Wines
Waitrose
The Wine Company
The Wine Society
The Wine Treasury
Peter Wylie Fine Wines
Yapp Brothers
Noel Young Wines

LONDON
Armit
Balls Brothers
Berkmann Wine Cellars
Berry Bros. & Rudd
Budgens
Corney & Barrow
Farr Vintners
Fortnum & Mason
Friarwood
Goedhuis & Co
Green & Blue
Handford Wines
Harvey Nichols
Haynes Hanson & Clark
Jeroboams
Lea & Sandeman
Moreno Wines

Philglas & Swiggot
Roberson
RSJ Wine Company
The Sampler
Selfridges
Waterloo Wine Co
Wimbledon Wine Cellar
Wine Rack
The Winery

SOUTH-EAST AND HOME COUNTIES
A&B Vintners
Berry Bros. & Rudd
Budgens
Butlers Wine Cellar
Les Caves de Pyrene
Flagship Wines
Hedley Wright
Maison du Vin
Quaff
Turville Valley Wines
Wine Rack

WEST AND SOUTH-WEST
Averys Wine Merchants
Bennetts Fine Wines
Berkmann Wine Cellars
Great Western Wine
Haynes Hanson & Clark
Hicks & Don
Old Chapel Cellars
Christopher Piper Wines
Reid Wines
Savage Selection
Peter Wylie Fine Wines
Yapp Brothers

EAST ANGLIA
Adnams
Budgens
Anthony Byrne
Cambridge Wine Merchants
Colchester Wine Co
Corney & Barrow
Seckford Wines
T & W Wines
Noel Young Wines

MIDLANDS
Bat & Bottle
Connolly's
deFINE Food and Wine
Gauntleys
Harvey Nichols
S H Jones
Nickolls & Perks
Noble Rot Wine Warehouses
Oxford Wine Co
Portland Wine Co
Selfridges
Stevens Garnier
Tanners

NORTH
Berkmann Wine Cellars
Booths
D Byrne
Great Northern Wine
Halifax Wine Co
hangingditch
Harvey Nichols
Martinez Wines
Nidderdale Fine Wines

Penistone Court
Playford Ros
Reserve Wines
Selfridges
Stainton Wines
Terroir Languedoc
Wright Wine Co

WALES
Ballantynes
Fingal-Rock
Terry Platt
Tanners

SCOTLAND
Corney & Barrow
Friarwood
Peter Green & Co
Harvey Nichols
Linlithgow Wines
Raeburn Fine Wines
Valvona & Crolla
Villeneuve Wines
WoodWinters

IRELAND
Direct Wine Shipments
James Nicholson
O'Briens
Winemark

CHANNEL ISLANDS
Sommelier Wine Co

FRANCE
ChateauOnline
Millésima
Wine & Beer World
The Wine Society